Broadcasting
in the United States

Innovative Challenge
and Organizational Control

Vincent Mosco

Georgetown University

ABLEX PUBLISHING CORPORATION
Norwood, New Jersey   07648

Library of Congress Cataloging in Publication Data

Mosco, Vincent.
  Broadcasting in the United States.

  (Communication and Information science)
  Based on the author's The regulation of broadcasting in the United States.
  Bibliography: p.
  Includes index.
  1. Broadcasting—United States. I. Title.
II. Series.
HE8689.8.M66   384.54'0973   78-16246
ISBN 0-89391-009-0

ABLEX Publishing Corporation
355 Chestnut Street
Norwood, New Jersey 07648

For Rose, Frank, Caroline, Leon, and Fred
Thanks

Contents

List of Tables

Preface

One of my first memories is hearing music come out of an old yellow radio sitting atop our refrigerator and wondering how all the players fit inside and why my father subjected us to "Make-Believe Ballroom" on Saturday morning. Make-believe. Television. I remember being struck by how big and clean everything looked. Television people lived in enormous houses (with staircases *inside*) that were spotlessly clean—as my mother would say, "You could eat off their floors." No cockroaches in TV land. No, this wasn't my Mulberry Street—well, anyway, Bishop Sheen said *I* would go to heaven—every week, he'd write it on the blackboard, during his TV show.

My involvement with radio and TV began in the same sense that I began, as if we were born together. Especially television: I ate and watched TV, read and watched TV, fought and watched TV, talked and watched TV (except when my father was watching and then we could only talk during commercials, or else). Some people vividly remember their first day at school; my most vivid memory as a six-year-old is getting dressed up in a pink shirt and bright blue slacks (to make a better impression before the new *color* TV cameras) and cheering under the direction of Buffalo Bob in Howdy Doody's Peanut Gallery. Television. It was there when I was sick, depressed, elated, bored—*there,* like no thing or no one else.

So when you grow up, what else do you write about? Actually, in a real sense, this book is not explicitly about TV; early on (perhaps it was that first APPLAUD/LAUGH sign) I learned that while television pictures a world, it was people, powerful people, who brought us television—who decided what we see and, more importantly, what we don't see. This book focuses on the fate of attempts to expand the radio/television world—on innovations that carried the hope of remaking that world only to be weakened by the structure that governs it. Specifically, I show how the regulatory system has helped maintain the dominance of AM radio and VHF television stations—and the profits of the companies that own these stations—at the expense of such innovations as FM radio, UHF, cable, and subscription television. I conclude by addressing two questions: Will such dominance continue? How can it be reversed?

My research on broadcasting began in the summer of 1973 when I worked as a graduate research assistant for Daniel Bell of Harvard's Sociology Department. I prepared a number of reports on information technologies and in the process was struck by how new developments in this area have been controlled—a first look at what broadcasting could be and why it wasn't. In the following year I wrote a doctoral dissertation proposal on the Federal Communications Commission and broadcasting with the help of Tony Oettinger, Director of the Program on Information Resources Policy at Harvard. My thesis, *The Regulation of Broadcasting in the United States: A Comparative Analysis** was completed with the support, direction, and prodding of Bell, Oettinger, and their colleague at Harvard, Christopher Jencks. I thank all three for their perceptive comments and general encouragement. I would also like to thank the many people whose interviews and comments on earlier drafts of this book guided me through a maze of complex dockets and baffling procedures. The final version of this book was completed in two very different worlds: while I was Chair of the Sociology Department at the University of Lowell and while a research fellow with the White House Office of Telecommunications Policy. I especially want to thank my students and sociology co-workers at Lowell who have been a source of support and joy and those at OTP who try—despite everything.

VINCENT MOSCO

---

*Cambridge, Mass: Harvard University Program on Information Technologies and Public Policy, 1975.

1
Introduction: Frustrated Hopes

In 1945 people were hailing FM radio as the "second chance" to create a broadcasting service both rich in diversity and free of commercialism—thirty years later it is merely a secondary service. In 1952 the FCC saw UHF television as a major competitor to the network-dominated VHF service—today UHF stations continue to lose money, to mirror VHF programming, and to be considered a waste of spectrum space. In 1965 cable television was called the Golden Antenna—many investors and subscribers have since come to feel that the antenna was made of fool's gold. In 1964 subscription television was the new medium most likely to succeed—today it is still struggling to get off the ground.

What happened? What has turned the optimistic forecasts about these broadcast market innovations into depressing chronicles of what might have been? This book tries to answer this question and, by doing so, illuminate the workings of one of the all too hidden federal regulatory agencies essential to the exercise of state power in America—the Federal Communications Commission. In the course of investigating the bureaucratic dynamics that mark the Commission's regulation of broadcasting we meet a varied cast of players, including such veterans of these wars as the broadcasting networks, the Congressional Commerce Committees, and those whose activity has grown in only recent years—for example, the Executive, the courts, and consumer groups. Their roles in this performance not only provide insight into the fate of these innovations, but also help us to understand why the structure of the dominant media in this country—radio and television—has been maintained in essentially the same form for several decades, despite the many proposals to reform the FCC since shortly after the Commission began its work. (See Table 1.1.)

Of course, there have been many studies on the general topic of broadcast

TABLE 1.1
Proposals to Reform the FCC[a]

1934   Special American Bar Association Committee on Administrative Law
  —abolish independent regulatory commissions and shift all but their specifically judicial work to Executive Branch bureaus
  —place judicial functions in an administrative court

1936   E. Pendleton Herring, *Federal Commissioners*
  —appoint more people to commission with industry experience

1937   President Roosevelt's Committee on Administrative Management
  —define FCC decision-making standards more clearly
  —shift administrative tasks of commissions to Executive Branch departments and make these departments responsible to a bureau headed by one person

1941   Attorney General's Committee on Administrative Procedure
  —clearly delegate functions and authority within each agency
  —establish a separate unit of hearing officers within each commission and provide for appeals of their decisions to the commission chairman
  (this report provided the basis for the Administrative Procedure Act of 1946)

1941   Robert Cushman, *Independent Regulatory Commissions*
  —separate executive from judicial functions in commissions, assigning executive work to Executive Branch departments and judicial work to an administrative court

1949   The First Hoover Commission
  —assign executive functions that are not specifically "regulatory" to the Cabinet
  —FCC staff should be organized along functional (broadcasting, common carrier, etc.) rather than professional (legal, technical, accounting, etc.) lines
  (a 1952 amendment to the Communications Act reorganized part of the FCC staff into functional bureaus)

1951   President Truman's Communication Policy Board
  —make the Commission's policy standards more specific
  —establish a long-range planning capacity at the FCC

1955   The Second Hoover Commission
  —remove judicial functions from commissions and place these functions within courts of general jurisdiction and special administrative courts

1959   Ronald Coase, "The Federal Communications Commission"
  —Congress should direct the FCC to auction off broadcasting licenses to the highest bidder

1959   Bernard Schwartz, *The Professor and the Commissions*
  —insulate the FCC from Executive Branch control by allowing the FCC to submit its budget directly to Congress (rather than through the Bureau of the Budget, now the Office of Management and Budget) and prohibit the President from removing an FCC Chairman

1960   Landis Commission Report to President-Elect Kennedy
  —extend FCC Commissioner tenure to ten years
  —authorize White House staff members to oversee regulatory agencies
  —create an administrative court for commissions

1962   Henry Friendly, *The Federal Administrative Agencies*
  —each decade an appropriate Congressional subcommittee should review all laws applying to a particular commission
  —create more specific standards for the FCC than those contained in the Communications Act

1962   Booz, Allen, and Hamilton, *Organization and Management of the FCC*

TABLE 1.1 *cont.*

    —the FCC needs more money and staff, but most importantly a better definition of standards

1964   Newton Minow, *Equal Time*
    —assign judicial functions of the FCC to an administrative court
    —assign executive functions of the FCC to a single administrator appointed by the President

1969   President Johnson's Task Force on Telecommunications
    —create an Executive Branch agency and assign it general responsibility for allocating the radio spectrum
    —the FCC should continue to license operators within spectrum areas assigned by this Executive agency

1970   Nicholas Johnson, *How to Talk Back to Your Television Set*
    —strengthen the organization of consumer interests by establishing a Citizen's Commission on Communications with the authority to appear as an advocate for the public interest before the FCC

1971   Walter Emery, *Broadcasting and Government*
    —lengthen the tenure of FCC Commissioners to ten or twelve years
    —increase the FCC's information-gathering capacity

1971   President Nixon's Advisory Council on Executive Organization
    —reduce the size of the FCC from seven to five Commissioners
    —the FCC is the only independent commission that should retain the collegial structure to insure broad-based deliberation and a non-partisan environment

1971   Brookings Institution Report: *Reforming Regulation*
    —possible options reported in this work:
      —independence with Presidential oversight
        —authorize the President to make general rules and policies for commissions through the use of executive orders
      —a regulatory czar
        —adopt Rexford Tugwell's New Deal proposal to create a second Vice President responsible for government regulation
      —legislative reform
        —eliminate the formal procedural requirements of the Administrative Procedure Act
      —constituent representative
        —assign each position on a regulatory commission to a representative of a particular interest

1972   Sidney W. Head, *Broadcasting in America*
    —the FCC should develop better standards, particularly for station licensing and renewals

1973   Erwin G. Krasnow and Harry M. Shooshan, "Congressional Oversight"
    —increase the Congressional oversight capacity by providing more staff and funding to the committees responsible for reviewing the FCC's work
    —increase the staff and funding of the FCC
    —develop more meaningful standards and guidelines for agency performance

1973   Roger G. Noll, Merton J. Peck, and John J. McGowan, *Economic Aspects of Television Regulation*
    —the FCC needs a new legislative mandate specifying the following:
      —broadcasters should be given the same first amendment freedoms regarding program content and quality as the print media
      —competition should replace localism as the primary broadcasting standard

TABLE 1.1

—the FCC's broadcast licensing concern should be limited to engineering and other technical aspects of spectrum management

1973 Rolla E. Park (ed.), *The Role of Analysis in Regulatory Decisionmaking*
—the FCC needs to increase its analysis and planning capability

1974 Henry Geller, "A Modest Proposal to Reform the Federal Communications Commission."
—decrease the number of FCC Commissioners to five
—extend Commissioners' tenure to fifteen years and bar reappointment
—do not allow Commissioners to work for the Communications industry until ten years after their tenure with the FCC is completed
—increase the quality of FCC Commissioners
—eliminate hearing procedures when facts are not disputed and use written submissions
—as suggested by former FCC Chairman Dean Burch:
—create two divisions at the FCC along these lines:
—broadcast/cable
—common carrier/safety and special services
—assign each division to half of the Commission
—the Chair would be responsible for convening the entire Commission on issues that overlap the divisions

1975 Committee for Economic Development, *Broadcasting and Cable Television*
—confer FCC adjudicatory functions to a new communications court following the pattern of the U. S. Tax Court when it was part of the Executive Branch
—the President should appoint judges for twelve year terms with Senate approval
—Congress and the FCC should strengthen the Office of Plans and Policy particularly by staffing the Office with more economists, engineers, attorneys, and social scientists

1975 Congressman Torbert Macdonald's Bill to Reform the FCC
—reduce the Commission size from seven to five
—increase the tenure of Commissioners from seven to ten years
—double the amount of staff assistance for each Commissioner
—require Commissioners to keep a record of contacts with lobbying groups
—make all meetings public unless it is determined by a majority vote of the Commission that a public meeting would be contrary to the public interest
—have the FCC go directly to Congress for appropriations rather than through the Office of Management and Budget
—make the President's designation of a Chairman subject to Senate approval
—have the FCC provide Congress with immediate access to documents and publish a quarterly rather than an annual report

1978 House Communications Subcommittee Proposed Communications Act Rewrite
—replace FCC with 5 member Communications Regulatory Commission
—limit CRC members to one 10 year term
—limit CRC regulation only "to the extent marketplace forces are deficient"
—deregulate radio and grant indefinite license terms
—grant indefinite TV licenses after 10 years
—set license fees for spectrum use
—abolish federal regulation of cable TV
—create independent executive branch National Telecommunications Agency

―――

*a*Included are proposals that apply to all independent commissions as well as to the FCC.

regulation, as well as some on the specific cases that this book examines. However, as Krasnow and Longley (1973) noted in their work on broadcast regulation:

> It is remarkable that the independent regulatory commissions, and in particular, the F.C.C., have never been subject to vigorous, analytical examination. . . . One looks in vain for studies of independent regulatory commissions which approach their inquiry with theoretical and conceptual vigor. (p. 73)

While this may be a bit overstated, the review of the literature in Chapter 2 does indicate that, with few exceptions, studies of broadcasting innovations[1] have focused on describing individual cases. Many of these studies are informative chronicles of events in these specific cases and, in some instances, interesting explanations have been offered. However, there is a real need to go beyond building on these case studies by comparing decision-making processes and outcomes across cases.

The need for comparative analysis in this area has been expressed rather well by Le Duc (1973) in his study of cable television. According to him,

> . . . while each specific agency action relating to innovative challenge might be explained in terms of its own unique facts, a comparision of a substantial number of decisions concerning similar types of challenges over an extended period of time might reveal significant parallels in approach and resolution transcending any explanation involving coincidental consistency, the tactics of a particular coalition of opponents, or the attitudes of a specific administration. (p. viii)

This report is basically an attempt to discover those "significant parallels in approach and resolution" that transcend the particular circumstances of each case and that thereby can increase our understanding of a government agency charged with the regulation of a rapidly changing and very powerful industry.

Specifically, the following ideas are given particular attention:

1. A useful way to understand decision-making processes in the four cases is to consider them as conservative responses induced by a complex environment. That is, decision-makers respond to complexity by imposing on the multiplicity of potential future variables a unifying simplicity rooted in preserving the status quo—a status quo generally supported by dominant interests. It is typically only a major disruption that leads to any measure of fundamental reassessment.

2. This conservative response has led to similar outcomes in each of the four cases, i.e., each innovation has developed into a role ancillary to the dominant commercial broadcasting system.

---

[1] I am aware that cable television cannot strictly be considered a "broadcasting" innovation. It was for this reason that my initial reference was to "innovations in the broadcasting market." The phrase "broadcasting innovation" is used as a shorthand for the latter throughout this analysis.

3.   While AM radio and VHF television continue to dominate, the FCC continues to absorb much of the criticism of those dissatisfied with the system.

These ideas illuminate Commission decision-making, suggest a reevaluation of reform proposals, and lead to the consideration of alternatives. Chapter 10 addresses reform proposals, stressing recommendations intended to broaden the base of Commission decision-making and to create a structure for systematically reviewing the Commission's activities.

It is important to recognize that this book is limited to one sphere of FCC activity, namely, broadcast regulation. It does not explicitly treat the Commission's responsibility to regulate the interstate rates and services of telephone and telegraph common carrier companies, predominantly AT&T. However, conclusions drawn from the area of broadcasting innovations should be useful to those interested in suggestions for the reform of regulation in general.

It should furthermore be understood that this book is not concerned with the entirety of the FCC's role in broadcast regulation. It does not explicitly address the licensing of stations and the review of program content. Whereas these are doubtless important FCC functions, the report concentrates on FM radio, UHF television, CATV, and STV for two primary reasons:

1.   Decision-making on these cases spans the full history of the FCC. FM became an issue in the radio industry in the early 1930s, and decision-making in all four areas continues to this day (see the Appendix beginning on p. 133).

2.   The comparison of decision-making processes and outcomes is faciliated by concentrating on innovations in one area. In this book it is the allocation of spectrum space in the broadcasting market.

The first chapter presents an overview of two contrasting though connected characteristics that have marked the history of broadcasting in the United States: the rapidity of the system's growth and the amount of criticism directed at it. This sets the context for a discussion of possible approaches to comparative analysis, approaches that are then used to help explain decision-making processes and outcomes in the four specific cases. Evidence from these cases is then applied to a review of policy options and their likely consequences for the regulation of radio and television services in the United States.

2
The Historical Context: Growth and Criticism

In a recent review article a British journalist (Smith, 1974) commented that "Everyone hates American television, apart from the people who watch it" (p. 713). Although the precise accuracy of this statement might be subject to challenge, it is certainly true that two of the characteristics that have significantly marked the history of broadcasting in the United States have been its rapid growth and the extensive criticism directed at the system.

SIXTY YEARS OF GROWTH

The Music Box

It was less than sixty years ago that David Sarnoff, then an assistant manager of the American Marconi Company, proposed the development of a "Radio Music Box" which, he claimed, would "make radio a 'household utility' in the same sense as the piano or phonograph" (Archer, 1938, pp. 112–13). Just six years later, in 1922, after the use of radio in World War I had lessened initial skepticism and after American Marconi had become the Radio Corporation of America, Sarnoff's novel idea became a commercial reality. From 1922 to 1925 the percentage of American households with radios grew from 0.2 to 10.1; from 1922 to 1926 the value of receivers increased from $5 million to $100 million (Schiller, 1970, p. 24).

The Nets

In 1926 another idea of Sarnoff's was realized with the development of a major instrument of broadcast industry growth and control—the network. A year before this Sarnoff had suggested putting "all stations of all parties into a broadcasting company which can be made self-supporting and probably revenue producing, the telephone company to furnish wires as needed" (Archer, 1939, p. 184).

A year later RCA, General Electric, and Westinghouse agreed to stop competing with one another and by pooling their various patents formed the National Broadcasting Company. The vital link among the parties and their stations was literally provided through a deal with AT&T by which the latter would lease lines for the new network. In 1927 NBC split into two national networks, the "Red" and the "Blue." Within two decades the latter would become the American Broadcasting Company. Also in 1927, a second eminent figure in the history of broadcasting, William Paley, linked together another group of stations under his Columbia Phonograph Broadcasting System to form what is now CBS. Thus, less than a decade into its commercial growth, the foundation was substantially laid for the development of broadcasting into a national network system.

The "Life Blood"

While the radio industry felt the economic impact of the Great Depression in the early 1930s, broadcasting continued to grow throughout that decade: The $200 million spent on radio sets in 1932 grew to $350 million in 1934. (Broadcasting Publications, 1939, p. 11). Radio quickly became an escape from the daily misery of struggling to survive. As the number of radios proliferated, network executives and owners of their affiliated stations increasingly turned to a new means of generating revenue—advertiser-sponsored programming. This development marked a major change from the early days of broadcasting. For in the twenties the idea of using advertising to finance the broadcasting system had been viewed with scorn or not considered at all. For example, the initial issue of *Radio Broadcast* (1922) magazine contained several suggestions for financing the new medium, including endowment by wealthy individuals and local financing through tax revenues, but no mention was made of advertising. The Radio Act of 1927 made merely one oblique reference to advertising by stipulating that material broadcast for a consideration be "announced as paid for or furnished, as the case may be, by such person, firm, company, or corporation." An early AT&T proposal (Barnouw, 1966, pp. 107–08) for "toll broadcasting" was considered by the editors of two trade journals to be "mercenary" and "positively offensive." Nevertheless, this experiment in commercial radio, begun by AT&T in the 1920s and centered on its primary station, WEAF in New York, became the model for the establishment of sponsored network broadcasting (Banning, 1946). Quite simply, once it became clear to owners that this would be the most lucrative way to finance the system, they used their power to overcome all opposition including that of Herbert Hoover who, as Secretary of Commerce, pleaded with broadcasters in a 1924 address (cited in Young, 1924) that:

> If a speech by the President is to be used as meat in a sandwich of two patent medicine advertisements, there will be no radio left.   (p. 248)

Radio not only survived patent medicine advertisements, it thrived on them: In 1938 sponsors spent over $150 million for broadcast time primarily with the 260 stations affiliated with NBC and CBS (Barnouw, 1968, p. 89; U.S. FCC, 1941, pp. 30–31).[1] Advertising was certainly becoming what radio manufacturer Harold La Fount (cited in Taylor, 1934) called "the life blood of the industry" (pp. 3–4).

International Growth

World War II slowed the economic growth of broadcasting in the United States, particularly that of such newcomers as frequency modulation radio and television. Nevertheless, as during World War I, certain aspects of broadcasting were able to grow even more rapidly than would be expected in peacetime. For example, the use of FM radio in the war sped its technical development. The war also gave rise to expanded uses of broadcasting, such as the establishment of an international broadcast news service that helped extend American dominance abroad.

The Picture Box and a Radio Resurgence

The 1950s were marked by the incredible growth of the television industry. At the start of the decade less than 4 million American households or 9% of all families had television sets (*Television Factbook:* 1973–74, p. 77-a). Only nine years later 86% of all families or 43 million households had televisions (*Television Factbook:* 1973–74, p. 77-a). As of 1975 over 68 million households (97% of the total) contained television sets (70% of which broadcast in color) that are viewed for what has been estimated to be an average of more than six hours per day (*Television Factbook,* 1977, p. 66-a).[2]

Whereas home radio sales, undoubtedly influenced by the sharp growth of television, leveled off in the early 1950s, growth resumed in the sixties when annual sales of 20 million receivers were recorded. This growth continued

[1]There were a total of 660 stations operating in 1938.

[2]Writing in 1967, Caroline Meyer estimated that "the average child has watched four thousand hours of television before his first day of school." Former FCC Commissioner Nicholas Johnson has noted that this amounts to twice the number of instructional hours in four years of college. Cf. Schiller (1970, p. 152).

into the latter part of the decade when the 30 million mark was passed (*Television Factbook:* 1969–70, pp. 70-a, 78-a). By 1977, 7370 commercial AM and FM stations broadcast into the 98% of all American households equipped with radios (*Broadcasting Yearbook,* 1977, p. A-2).

In Perspective

The broadcasting industry, including both radio and television, now generates in excess of $6 billion in net annual revenues. (*Broadcasting Yearbook:* 1977, p. A-2). Of course, revenue figures alone do not establish the significance of the broadcasting system. As Noll, Peck, and McGowan (1973) have noted:

> American television is an average-sized industry. The combined annual revenue of television stations and networks is . . . about the same as such prosaic activities as the manufacture of paperboard boxes, cotton broadwoven fabrics, or canned fruits and vegetables. But, because they measure only the role television plays in advertising, these revenues grossly understate the importance of the industry, even for the economist. (p. 1)[3]

That importance can perhaps be better gauged by considering the variety and amount of criticism that has been directed at the system.

CRITICISM: THE BROADCASTING SYSTEM

Overly rooted in commercialism, dominated by a few large corporations, a cultural wasteland, insensitive to minority tastes—these are some of the major criticisms directed at broadcasting during the decades of its economic growth. What follows is a brief review of this attack.

The commercial basis of broadcasting has been a particularly strident focus of criticism from the earliest days of the industry. A 1922 article in *Radio Broadcast* (Jackson, 1922) magazine noted that:

> No one who reads this article will have to consider very long what broadcast advertising implies, before the presence of the difficulty becomes apparent enough. The very thought of such a thing growing to be common practice is sufficient to give any true radio enthusiast the cold shakes. (p. 72)

It was not only the "enthusiast" who got the "cold shakes" from the idea of advertising on the air; many others felt that the popularity of the system would dissipate were it to continue being financed by commercial advertising. Several calls were made in the 1920s for legislation prohibiting the use of radio for advertising (Bliven, 1924). No such ban was enacted but, as the Federal Radio Commission (the FCC's predecessor) began its work in 1927, chief among the recommendations it received was the abolition of so-called

[3]Even within the communications industry broadcasting is dwarfed by the telephone sector which generates over four times as much in annual revenues. Cf. Borchardt (1970).

"direct" advertising and the confinement of "indirect" advertising to the day-time hours (U.S. FRC, 1927).[4]

Growing commercialism was not the only source of criticism in broadcasting's first decade. A charge commonly heard today was made in 1924 when the Federal Trade Commission (cited in Barnouw, 1966) claimed that RCA, General Electric, Westinghouse, United Fruit, and AT&T had

> combined and conspired for the purpose of, and with the effect of, restraining competition and creating a monopoly in the manufacture, purchase and sale in interstate commerce of radio devices . . . and in domestic and transoceanic communications and broadcasting. (p. 162)[5]

Just a few years into its history the broadcasting system was criticized for being dominated by a few large corporations.

Criticism continued unabated into the 1930s, especially among members of Congress and educators who wanted a portion of the radio band reserved for noncommercial use. Particularly vocal among the former were Senator Burton K. Wheeler, who criticized the radio industry for having turned the airwaves into a "pawnshop," and Senator James Couzens, who made an unsuccessful attempt to force the Federal Radio Commission to limit advertising solely to an announcement of sponsorship (Barnouw, 1966, p. 243). Joy Elmer Morgan was one of the more outspoken critics representing educational interests. In a 1931 article (cited in Rorty, 1931) he criticized the "giving away of radio stations of untold value with no thought of compensation or no reservation, as in the case of the public domain, for the use of education" (p. 716).[6]

This decade was not without its concern for monopoly practices in the industry. This time it was the Justice Department deciding in 1930 to start antitrust action against RCA, General Electric, Westinghouse, and AT&T. Although the government was somewhat successful in disentangling the complicated interconnections among these companies, the outcome left RCA with near complete dominance over the industry. It controlled two networks, major manufacturing facilities, international ship-to-shore communications systems, and the majority of clear channel radio stations (stations whose signal can cover over a thousand miles at night because no stations are licensed within its frequency range over its potential geographical coverage area). This led to further criticism and court action into the next decade.

---

[4]While the distinction between direct and indirect advertising is somewhat vague, one can say that the former was generally used to indicate outright appeals for the purchase of a product, while indirect advertising was limited to announcing that a particular company was sponsoring a program. Direct advertising came to be defined more and more narrowly until by 1930 it was considered to mean only "stating prices." Anything else was indirect advertising and therefore suitable for broadcasting. Cf. U.S. Congress, Senate (1929–1930).

[5]Cf. U.S. Federal Trade Commission (1924).

[6]Cf. Rorty (1934).

The 1940s saw criticism of the broadcasting system coming from both the FCC as well as from a man who helped lay the technical foundation for the industry. In its 1941 *Report on Chain Broadcasting,* the FCC attacked the increasing concentration of programming control in the two major commercial networks. The order accompanying this report led to RCA's sale of its minor network, the Blue chain. The Commission's authority to issue such an order was upheld by the Supreme Court in 1942.[7] In 1946 the FCC published a report on the *Public Service Responsibility of Broadcast Licensees.* This report (US, FCC, 1946), also known as the "Blue Book," attacked the excessive amount of air time sold to advertisers and the paucity of locally produced programming. Charles Siepmann, formerly with the BBC and a member of the group who prepared the "Blue Book," was even more strident in his criticism of what he referred to as "the networks abdication to the advertisers" (Siepmann, 1946). He argued that "radio has become the drudge of advertising, selling itself to big business for a handsome price, identified with it body and soul, if any soul remains to it" (p. 191).

Also in 1946, Lee de Forest, who forty years earlier had developed the "Audion," a three-element vacuum tube, vehemently struck out against the system that he had helped to develop. In a letter to the convention of the National Association of Broadcasters (*Chicago Tribune,* October 28, 1946; cited in Barnouw, 1968), de Forest criticized the industry for what he felt it had done to his "child": "You have made of him a laughing stock to intelligence . . . . you have cut time into tiny segments called spots (more rightly stains) herewith the occasional fine program is periodically smeared with impudent insistence to buy and try" (p. 234).[8]

In the last twenty-five years, criticism has continued to parallel the growth of broadcasting, particularly the commercial television system. In addition to often cited statements, such as Newton Minow's characterization of television as a "vast wasteland" (*Broadcasting,* May 15, 1961, pp. 58–59) and former Vice-President Agnew's 1970 speech on network "censorship" are popular accounts that have largely focused on the commercial basis of broadcasting. Harry Skornia's (1965) *Television and Society,* Les Brown's (1971) *Television: The Business Behind the Box,* and Martin Mayer's (1972) *About Television* are good examples of the former.

Skornia concentrates on what he considers to be the contradiction between profitability and the public interest. He claims that the American system of broadcasting, "is what it is now because this form of broadcasting is most profitable to those who control it, not because it serves the public interest better than, or even as well as, any of a number of alternatives might" (p. 10). Brown focuses on the three major television networks, that is, what he calls

---

[7]*CBS v. U.S.,* 316 U.S. 407 (1942). *NBC v. U.S.,* 316 U.S. 447 (1942).
[8]de Forest repeats this theme throughout his autobiography (de Forest, 1950).

"the Three Rocks," and argues that their basic function is merely to bring potential buyers to advertisers: "In day-to-day commerce, television is not so much interested in the business of communications as in the business of delivering people to advertisers. People are the merchandise not the shows. The shows are merely the bait" (pp. 15–16). Finally, Mayer criticizes the system because it is completely dominated by "the mystical business of selling time" (p. 55).

The broadcasting system has met and continues to meet with strident criticism—while the profits grow. Perhaps one reason why they grow is that a good deal of the criticism is deflected by the institutions that regulate broadcasting—particularly the Federal Communications Commission.

CRITICISM: THE REGULATION OF BROADCASTING

In 1958 the staff of the Hoover Commission concluded its extensive analysis of the federal bureaucracy on this note: No agency of the federal government has been subjected to greater attack for failing to perform effectively, and no regulatory commission has undergone as much Congressional criticism and investigation as has the FCC (U.S. Commission, 1948). In his 1962 analysis of federal administrative agencies, Judge Henry Friendly argued that the FCC "has had a rather long turn at the whipping post" (p. 53). Echoing this in their 1973 work on the Commission, Krasnow and Longley contend that "perhaps no other Federal agency has been the subject of as much vilification and prolonged investigation. . ." (p. 58). Table 1.1 and a brief review of research on the FCC leave one with the impression that these remarks understate the case.

Restriction of Innovation

One focus of this criticism has been on the alleged restrictive influence that organizations such as the FCC have brought to bear on technological innovations. The Communications Act of 1934 stipulates that the Commission "study new uses for radio, provide for experimental uses of frequencies, and generally encourage the larger and more effective use of radio in the public interest" (section 303g). Some have claimed that the FCC has not at all lived up to this requirement.

In his book on regulatory reform, Noll (1971b) singles out the FCC along with the Interstate Commerce Commission for being among the most restrictive to change:

Regulatory agencies have delayed or prevented a number of technological changes that threatened either to shift a substantial business from one regulated firm or industry to

another or to result in substantially less profit for regulated firms generally. The agencies
most often guilty of such choices are the ICC and the FCC. . . . (p. 24)

Le Duc (1973), in his analysis of cable television regulation, considers this
restrictive influence as perhaps an inevitable feature of regulatory agencies
such as the FCC and therefore sees little hope in minor reform proposals, for
"unless any structural bias against technological competition is remedied
through modifications of the agency's regulatory process, each future advance
may be foredoomed to a series of restraints no less severe than those already
experienced by the cable medium" (p. ix). Nevertheless, he questions the in-
evitability of a restrictive policy in the broadcasting area—for here the Commission is in no way legally bound to maintain the industry's economic stabil-
ity as it is in the common carrier field where the Commission directly super-
vises rates and services.

The President's Advisory Council (1971) put a White House stamp on
this charge when it noted the tendency of the FCC and other regulatory agencies "to shield all regulated modes often without sufficient assessment of . . . efficiency factors that might intrinsically favor one of several
modes" (p. 71). Finally, writing in the *Federal Communications Bar Journal*
Spievack (1969) considers the Commission's failure to "promote technological innovation and progress" its "greatest criticism" (p. 177).

Since our concern is with the FCC's response to innovations in the broadcasting market, it is important to consider the basis of this criticism. Research
on the Commission suggests several possibilities.

External Pressure: Broadcasters and the Congress

Broadcast regulation has been criticized because certain organizations al-
legedly exercise excessive influence on the process. Some of the literature on
the FCC is directed at the extent to which the Commission has been overly
sympathetic to the interests of the broadcasting industry. As early as 1935,
Herring conveyed what has since become the belief of many analysts and critics when he wrote: "While talking in terms of public interest, convenience
and necessity, the Commission actually chose to further the ends of the commercial broadcasters" (p. 173). Just six years later Cushman (1941) echoed
this interpretation and applied it to both the FCC and its predecessor:

Neither the Radio Commission nor its successor, the Federal Communications Commission, has come to grips with the major policy problems which are involved in the regulation of the radio industry. The two commissions have followed the line of least resistance
and have assumed that what is best for the radio industry as a business enterprise must
also be best for the country. (p. 29)

The notion that the broadcasting industry exerts considerable influence on
the Commission's decision-making has been prominent in several recent

analyses. Noll (1971b) argues that this results in a rather unique definition of the public interest: The FCC's public interest goals seem "remarkably consistent" (p. 21) with the profitability goals of broadcasters.[9] This has also been noted by Geller (1975) who observes that the one clear problem that must be faced is agency overidentification with the industries regulated and by Moore (1973) who claims that "the peculiar vision . . . of regulators tends to be that whatever is good for the networks or the broadcasters is also good for the public" (p. 61).[10]

Several analysts have argued that this sort of pressure is actually effective only during a particular period in the development of a regulatory agency. In his book *The Great Crash*, Galbraith (1955) summarizes the life cycle of a regulatory agency:

> In youth they are vigorous, aggressive, evangelistic and even intolerant. Later they mellow, and in old age—after a matter of ten or fifteen years—they become, with some exceptions, either an arm of the industry they regulate or senile. (p. 171)

Bernstein explains specifically what he believes takes place in the latter part of the cycle. He argues that during "old age" the working agreement that an agency reaches with the regulated industries becomes so fixed that the agency has no creative energy left to mobilize against the industry (discussed in Krislov & Musolf, 1964, pp. 85–86). Schwartz (1959) adds that "in none of the regulatory agencies has this been more apparent than in the FCC" which is in an "ossified stage" (p. 127).[11]

Several attempts have been made to show that broadcast industry pressure has been particularly successful when efforts have been made to reorganize the FCC or when the Commission itself has tried to redirect its own policy. Examples include the Kennedy Administration's attempt to reorganize the FCC in 1961 (Brinton, 1962, p. 58) and the FCC proposal to limit commercial broadcast advertising time in 1963 (Krasnow & Longley, 1973, pp. 105-11).[12]

Some have claimed that a reason for the supposed success of broadcast industry pressure is the association of Commissioners with the industry prior to and/or after their FCC appointment. A study by Ross Eckert (1972, p. 104) of the White House Office of Telecommunications Policy indicates that 20% of Commissioners appointed between 1934 and 1972 came from the broadcasting

[9]Noll's colleagues at a Brookings Institution conference considered this to be a common problem of all regulatory agencies. They considered "the tendency of regulators to be too responsive to the interests of regulated industries as the main cause of undesirable regulatory policies and industry performance" (Noll, 1971b, p. 99).

[10]Geller emphasized this in an interview that I conducted with him in December 1974.

[11]Cf. Friendly (1962) and Jaffe (1954).

[12]While generally accepting the argument that the broadcasting industry exerts a great influence on the FCC, the authors point to the unique precedent in broadcasting that it was the industry itself that initiated its own regulation in the 1920s to bring order to a terribly chaotic system.

and newspaper industries. Defining association with the industry more broadly, Lichty (1961–62) observes that 24 of 43 members appointed to the Federal Radio Commission and the FCC up until 1961 "had some experience with broadcasting before becoming members of the Commission" (p. 30). Although there has been some difference of opinion about the recruitment *source* of Commissioners, there can be no dispute that a large number do take jobs in the communications industry *after leaving* the FCC. This has been noted in reports by Michael (1974, p. 262). Lichty (1961–62, p. 30), and most recently in data compiled by Noll, Peck, & McGowan (1973). Although the authors assert that "these data do not imply that FCC officials are corrupt," the data do "suggest that most of these people must find themselves—at least some of the time—in the difficult position of sorting out the public interest from their own interests as future employees of regulated firms" (pp. 123–24). See Table 2.1.

Others who agree with the industry pressure interpretation have been much less critical of the role of broadcasting companies. For example, Bernard Schwartz, who headed an investigation of regulatory agencies in the 1950s that led to resignations from the FCC, has written (Schwartz, 1959) that while there have undoubtedly been "constant efforts to influence the Commission,"

> the powers vested in the FCC are so tremendous, giving it virtually uncontrolled life-and-death authority over the broadcast industry, that those engaged in broadcasting simply cannot afford a Commission that is hostile to them. (p. 38)

Thus, while it is still the FCC–industry relationship that is the focus of attention, the positions are reversed with the Commission considered the dominant

TABLE 2.1
Affiliation of FCC Commissioners and Other Officials
with the Communications Industry, 1945–70[a]

Status of affiliation	Number of commissioners[b]	Number of other high-level staff[c]
Total number holding positions	33	32
Affiliation with Communications Industry		
Before FCC service	4	8
After FCC service	21	13
Never[d]	11	11

[a]Departure date 1945–70 (after Noll, Peck, & McGowan, 1973, p. 123).

[b]Three who were affiliated before and after are counted twice.

[c]Executive director, General Counsel, Chief engineer, bureau chiefs, chairman of review board, chief hearing examiner and chief of office of opinions and review, chief of reports and information.

[d]Includes three unknown who were not affiliated prior to FCC service.

force controlling the direction of the broadcasting industry. An attempt to justify the need for this relationship is provided by James Landis (1960) in his *Report on Regulatory Agencies to the President-Elect* prepared for the incoming Kennedy Administration. Here he notes that contacts between the FCC and industry "are frequently productive of intelligent ideas," whereas contacts with the public are considered to be "generally unproductive of anything except complaint," (p. 71). Former FCC Chairman Newton Minow echoed this statement (cited in Moore, 1973) and, in addition, considered it to be part of the "Catch-22" nature of Commission–industry relationships. According to him,

Those who make policy and regulate must necessarily have frequent contact with the industry in order to be well informed. Under the present system, the possibility of improper influence or at least of charges of such influence is always present. (p. 16)

It is thus claimed that in carrying out their regulatory responsibilities, Commissioners must put themselves in a position of having their decision-making influenced by the broadcasting industry.

Some have observed that this problem is rooted in the Commission's dependence on the industry for technical information. For example, the Hoover Commission (cited in Lessing, 1949, pp. 124–25) criticized the inadequacy of the Commission's technical staff and its consequent dependence on industry engineers for data and advice. A Congressional report (U.S. Congress, Senate, 1958a, pp. 221–26) pointed to the significance of industry advisory bodies that are created, often by the Commission itself, to advise the FCC on policy matters. The report claims that such bodies frequently take the place of independent long-range planning by the Commission itself.[13] Le Duc (1973) observes that this particular problem severely restrains the development of broadcasting innovations because "there is no effective information-gathering process within the FCC capable of providing the material necessary to evaluate the potential for public service of new communications techniques" (p. 28).

Next to the broadcasting industry, the Congress has received most attention as a major influence on FCC decision-making. Although the Senate is formally responsible for deciding on Presidential appointments to the Commission, both Houses, particularly through their respective Commerce Committees, oversee the FCC's budget and performance. On the latter function, Krasnow and Longley (1973, p. 58) claim that the FCC is preeminent among agencies subject to constant Congressional scrutiny. Furthermore, they consider matters to be complicated by the fact that, unlike the broadcasting industry, Congress is often quite vague about what it actually wants from the

[13]Discussed below is one of the more prominent of these advisory groups—the Radio Technical Planning Board. It was heavily involved with decision-making on radio and television in the late 1940s.

Commission. Consequently, "One of the tasks of the FCC, then, is to make crucial decisions when the *wishes* of Congress are quite unclear, but the pressure is very real" (p. 62). Laurence Laurent supports this view in his essay introducing Newton Minow's popular book *Equal Time* (1964). Laurent considers the frustrations of the FCC member who

> . . . may be admonished one day by the Chairman of the Senate Commerce Committee for being too aloof from members of the broadcasting industry. . . . In the very next session the same FCC member may be advised by the very same Congressman that he has gotten too close to the broadcasting industry. (pp. 277–78).

Minow himself claims that during his tenure as Commission Chairman he "heard from Congress as frequently as television commercials flash across the screen" (p. 36). Finally, in *Broadcasting and Government,* Walter Emery (1971, p. 395) criticizes the extent to which the FCC has been "investigation-ridden" by the Congress and particularly by the Commerce Committees in each House.[14]

Why such close Congressional scrutiny? Some argue that it is necessary to protect the symbiotic relationship between representatives and the major broadcasters (Krasnow & Longley, 1973, p. 56). This relationship is not primarily based on investments by members of Congress in the broadcasting industry: *Broadcasting* magazine (May 24, 1971, p. 58) reports that in the 92nd Congress only six Senators and nine Representatives had such investments. Rather, according to several analysts, it is based on the free provision of radio and television time to members of Congress. For example, Cary (1967) writes that:

> Vis-à-vis the FCC, the radio and television industry can, through its network and local stations, exert enormous political pressure. It controls access of members of Congress to the voters. The stations can support or oppose a candidate; they can offer free time and coverage. (p. 45)

Krasnow and Longley (1973, p. 56) report that over 60% of Congressional membership regularly makes use of this time; in return, stations are credited for public service programming.

The creation of the White House Office of Telecommunications Policy by the Nixon Administration began to shift some of the criticism of extra-agency governmental influence to the executive branch. Several observers saw this as a major threat to the FCC's independence (e.g., Spievack, 1969; Herbers, 1973). Finally, the growing influence of citizens groups is beginning to worry some people. According to an article in the *Federal Communications Bar Journal,* one commentator (Padden, 1972) complains that such groups

---

[14]Brinton (1962, p. 52) argues that these investigations have led to few constructive changes since, in order to retain control, Congress has never questioned the basic soundness of the Commission form.

"threaten to take a medium with the proven ability to bring people together and use it to divide them" (p. 109).

Despite these recent developments, the broadcasting industry and the Congress continue to be viewed as the major external influences on FCC decision-making.

Too Independent

Another major basis for criticizing the Commission comes from those who concentrate not on external pressures, but rather on the Commission's statutory independence. These analysts generally argue that independence tends to separate regulatory agencies such as the FCC from the technical and political support needed to execute its policies with some measure of efficiency and consistency. For example, the President's Advisory Council (1971) criticized regulatory agencies in general because such organizations are ". . . not sufficiently accountable for their actions to either the Congress or the President because of the degree of their independence and remoteness in practice from those constitutional branches of government. . ." (p. 4). Bernstein (1955) expresses a similar concern: regulatory commissions suffer a rapid "decay" because they are isolated by law from "energizing" sources of political support (p. 88–90). He considers ". . . the single most important characteristic of regulation by commission . . . the failure to grasp the need for political support and leadership for the success of regulation in the public interest" (p. 101). Following this line of thinking with specific reference to the FCC, Brinton (1962) has claimed that it is "isolation from presidential leadership and control . . . lack of continuous or effective legislative guidance . . . as well as the evident apprehension of the courts" that has led to the FCC's failures. More significantly, he argues, the independence of the Commission has contributed to the removal of "significant issues of policy from the fullest possible discussion and debate" (pp. 1, 19–20, 562).

In conclusion, some have criticized the Commission not for being "captured" by other organizations but, quite to the contrary, for being too independent or separated from important segments of the political and economic arenas.

The Critique of Localism

Another source of criticism has been the Commission's alleged attachment to the goal of localism or the idea that broadcast stations should be established in as many locations as possible with the control of both ownership and programming concentrated at the local level. Whereas some claim that the standard of localism is actually a legislative mandate emanating from both the 1927 Radio Act and the Communications Act of 1934, and therefore ought to be considered simply as another source of Congressional influence,[15] most treat it as a goal to which the FCC has become independently attached.

In their work on the economics of broadcast regulation, Noll, Peck, and McGowan (1973) support the latter perspective. In addition, they contend that ". . . the record shows little willingness to subordinate the local service obligation to any of the other objectives" (p. 100). Head (1972) has been particularly critical about the way in which the Commission has administered the local service principle. He contends that:

> Some forty years of licensing nominally based squarely on an obligation to ascertain and satisfy local community needs had apparently not sufficed to build up an understanding either of what this obligation means or of a modus operandi for meeting it. (p. 458)

Mayer (1972) has considered this to be true for television, for "brushing aside sporadic incidents of government resistance" (p. 279) television has developed into a national service controlled by the three major networks and group station owners. Noll and his colleagues have argued more specifically with reference to television that concern for localism has limited the opportunities for achieving other values that Commissioners and policy analysts have sought. They observe that Commission attachment to localism has ironically contributed to cross-media concentration, because often the most qualified local groups seeking a television station license have been local newspaper or radio stations. In addition, they contend that the concept of localism has protected the three-network system and therefore restrained competition by preventing major group stations, such as those controlled by Metromedia and Westinghouse, from organizing into additional major networks (Noll et al, 1973, pp. 105–06). In this same vein, the Rostow Report, commissioned during the Johnson Administration, claimed that the standard of localism has hampered efforts to achieve a diversified system of programming because it has led the Commission to prohibit the establishment of powerful regional stations that might provide more signals and a wider program choice to most viewers (President's Task Force, 1969, Chapter 7, p. 12).

Criticism of the Commission's commitment to localism has also been applied to radio. According to Le Duc (1973):

> Two decades of the radio regulatory policy of constantly sacrificing program coverage for local service had resulted in a broadcast system in which one family in six still remained without nighttime entertainment or news while urban dwellers received multiple channels of music, covering areas, not communities with homogenous, nationally distributed recorded programming. (p. 54)

Several attempts have been made to explain the Commission's attachment to localism by those who consider it to be more than adherence to a statutory

---

[15]Cf. Comaner and Mitchell (1972, p. 181) and Cotter (1960, pp. 316–22).

mandate. Noll et al. (1973) contend that it stems from the Commission's peculiar vision of the station owner ". . . as a kind of latter-day Mark Twain who understands the needs and concerns of his community in an imaginative and sensitive way. Given this conception, the ownership of the local station is crucial" (p. 104). Goldin, on the other hand, argues that it is important to distinguish between localism as an *entrepreneurial* and a *service* policy. According to him, the Commission has administered localism as the former—a means for getting more people into the broadcasting business. Understood in that sense, localism is a policy that has been administered with some success. Goldin does not believe that the Commission has ever really considered a local *service* policy to be a serious goal. (Interview, Boston, 1974) Finally, there are those, like Schwartz (1959), who consider localism, even as understood in its entrepreneurial sense, to be of little more than ideological significance to the Commission. According to him,

> Despite the clear desirability of giving stations to local entrepreneurs, which the FCC itself has constantly stressed, in a number of cases in recent years the Commission has held against local owners and preferred applicants wholly owned by outside interests. (p. 152)

The Bureaucratic Commission

The FCC has not only been criticized for being excessively sympathetic to outside interests and for its attachment to an unworkable policy, but also because of its internal operations. The 1971 report of the President's Advisory Council summarized this line of thinking rather well. The Council claimed that while "it would be easy to attribute dissatisfaction with the performance of regulatory commissions . . . to overidentification with the industry regulated" (p. 31), it considered this to be merely a symptom of a more far-reaching problem. According to the Council,

> . . . obsolete organization forms limit the effectiveness of . . . commissions in responding to economic, technological, structural and social change. Inappropriate regulatory structures and cumbersome procedures impose burdens that impede good public service, sound financial and operational planning, and adjustment to changes in growing industries—contrary to the purposes of regulations. (p. 4)

The following are several specific bases upon which the FCC has been criticized for its internal operations.

1. The Collegial Form. The FCC is structured along collegial lines, i.e., power is shared relatively equally among the seven members. This organizational structure has been the focus of critics for many years. More than forty years ago Herring (1936a) argued that the collegial form provides the FCC and other regulatory agencies with a "cloak of anonymity" (p. 1) that shields it from public scrutiny. This has recently been noted by the President's Advisory Council as well as by the former head of the FCC's Common Carrier Bureau, Dr. Bernard Strassburg, (Interview, Washington, D.C., 1974).

2. Commission Turnover Rate. Some have contended that the FCC's difficulties stem, at least in part, from the high turnover rate of Commissioners. According to Lichty's research (1962b, pp. 23–24), few Commissioners ever complete a full seven year term—the average is about 4.5 years. He considers this too short a period of time for people to develop the expertise to regulate effectively.

3. Too Many Lawyers. E. Pendleton Herring also singled out in 1936 "the predominance of lawyers among our commissioners" that he felt could not be justified by the type of work that they are called upon to do (Herring, 1936a, p. 42). To this day, what has been considered an overabundance of lawyers and the need for more economic expertise are still major concerns of critics (Park, 1973, p. 38; interview with Hyman Goldin, 1974).

Krasnow (himself a communications lawyer) and Longley contend that a major problem stemming from the predominance of lawyers serving on the FCC is a general tendency to view problems in "narrow legal terms" rather than in their broader social context (Krasnow & Longley, 1973, p. 27). More specifically, this leads to an overemphasis on the use of what they consider to be a cumbersome and unfair case method: cumbersome because deciding each case on an individual basis consumes time and scarce resources, and unfair because ad hoc decision-making results in different outcomes for similar cases.

4. Too Little Money. Several analysts have claimed that a principal cause of the Commission's administrative deficiencies is insufficient funding for a workload that a report for the Bureau of the Budget termed "of staggering proportions" (Booz, Allen, & Hamilton, 1962, p. 1). The budgetary problem was illustrated rather clearly in a speech by Nicholas Johnson at a meeting of the Federal Communications Bar Association in 1968 (cited by Krasnow & Shooshan, 1973):

> The FAA spends as much on *communications research* as the FCC's total annual budget; the Navy spends five times the FCC's annual budget doing cost-effectiveness studies of the communications system of one ship type; Bell Labs has a budget over 15 times that of the FCC. (p. 308)

5. Conflicting Demands. Some claim that the FCC's external difficulties stem from the fact that Commissioners and staff often work at cross-purposes. Specifically, it has been argued that the Commission has a difficult time coordinating its activities because it was set up both to promote as well as to regulate the communications industry (Bernstein, 1955, pp. 254–56; Fainsod, Gordon, & Palamountain, 1959, pp. 299–300; U.S. Congress, House, 1960, pp. 6–8). Conflicts arise because it is required both to support experimentation and allocate frequencies, while at the same time adjudicate disputes among different segments of the industry.

6. Capture by Staff or Commissioners.   There are those who contend that the Commission could not function well with or without such conflicting demands as promotion and regulation. For example, both Louis Jaffe and James Q. Wilson argue that instead of viewing regulatory agencies like the FCC as industry-oriented, it is best to consider them as "regulation-oriented." According to Wilson (1971),

> They are in the regulation business, and regulate they will, with or without a rationale. If the agencies have been 'captured' by anybody, it is probably by their staffs who have mastered the arcane details of rate setting and license granting. (p. 48)[16]

Le Duc argues that staff control becomes particularly pronounced in the face of new technological developments within the regulated industry largely because new technology represents a threat to the power base of a staff—a base built on expertise vis-à-vis the established technology (Le Duc, 1969, pp. 102–03).

How is this power exercised? Thurston (Interview, Boston, 1975) claims that one way is through the staff's definition of problem areas to be considered by Commission members; another is the use of the bureaucracy itself as a protective device by creating for Commissioners, in the words of Newton Minow (1964), "a jungle of procedural red tape" (p. 8). In these ways the staff can curtail the growth of any new development that might threaten its power base.

While agreeing that using the bureaucracy as a protective device is a problem with the FCC, several analysts have disagreed with this specific interpretation. Both Schwartz and Head criticize Commission members rather than the staff for this problem. According to Schwartz (1959),

> The Commission juggles its criteria in particular cases so as to reach almost any decision it wishes and then orders its staff to draw up reasons to support the decision. (p. 191)

Head (1972) provides a concrete example of how this operates specifically in relations between Commissioners and the Office of Opinions and Review:

> The Office of Opinions once dutifully wrote up a hundred-page opinion justifying a competitive television grant, only to have the Commission change its mind and award the license to another applicant. The Office went back to work and came up with another hundred pages, equally convincing in reaching an opposite conclusion. (p. 449)

7. Failure to Analyze and Plan.   Perhaps the greatest amount of criticism directed at the Commission's internal operations has focused on the failure to analyze problems comprehensively, implement decisions efficiently, and develop policies for the long-term growth of a national communications system. This argument has been particularly prominent in government reports on the FCC over the last 35 years.

---

[16]For Jaffe's position see Krislov and Musolf (1964, pp. 128–33, 231–39).

In the first major governmental investigation of the FCC, conducted by the Presidential Committee on Administrative Management (1937), attention was concentrated on the Commission's inability to formulate "integrated government policy," (pp. 32–33, 39–40). In 1948, after an extensive investigation, the Hoover Commission (U.S. Commission, 1948) arrived at a similar conclusion,

> The Commission has been found to have failed both to define its primary objective intelligently and to make policy determinations required for effective and expeditious administration. (p. 10)

The Hoover Commission study claimed that the inadequacies of the FCC's staff have not only forced the Commission to depend on broadcast industry engineers for data and advice, but it has also contributed to a "lack of order, continuity, consistency, long-range planning and political stature in the commission itself."

This emphasis on the inability to develop general policies and to administer them efficiently was underscored by another Presidential body in 1951. After brushing aside the argument that FCC difficulties stem from the amount of work before it, the President's Communication Policy Board (1951) claimed that the Commission was unable to ". . . deal effectively with the workload before it because it has not formulated the broad policies to guide its decisions and thereby expedite handling of cases. . ." (p. 195).

There has been no Presidential monopoly on explicit criticism of the FCC from this perspective. A task force report to the Senate Commerce Committee completed in 1958 (known as the "Bowles Report") arrived at similar conclusions in concentrating on a Commission tendency toward expediency rather than efficiency and comprehensiveness (U.S., Congress, Senate, 1958a, p. 9).

Three reports commissioned by the Executive Branch in the 1960s have followed the pattern of their predecessors. Reporting to President-elect Kennedy, the Landis Commission viewed the FCC as unable to deal with its problems efficiently, in both the long and short term. It concluded that the FCC was "incapable of policy planning" as well as of "dispensing within a reasonable period of time the business before it" (Landis, 1960, p. 53).[17] Two years later, a report for the Bureau of the Budget (Booz et al., 1962) arrived at similar conclusions. While the report admonishes the Congress for failing to provide the Commission with needed funding, it concentrates on the lack of rational administration at the FCC. It concludes on an all too familiar pessimistic note:

> Ensuing years will see the Commission engage in an increasingly futile attempt to meet its statutory responsibilities unless, by conscious effort, it is able to establish more clearly its objectives and criteria, to obtain support requisite to its towering responsibilities and to maximize the efficiency of its administrative machinery. . . . (p. 2)

[17]Landis later indicated that it was "the complexity and prolixity of existing procedures" which helped defeat the reform measures recommended by his commission. Cf. Landis in (Krislov & Musolf, 1964, pp. 87–91).

In 1969 the President's Task Force on Communications focused more specifically on the FCC's failure to develop an analytic capability. It points out that despite internal reorganization and incorporation of computer facilities, the Commission still lacked the ". . . capacity for analysis of major issues having technical, economic and regulatory policy dimensions, even when these issues are central to its regulatory responsibilities" (Chap. 9, p. 24).

Two recent examples of this line of criticism come from the Nixon administration. The 1971 report of the Presidential Council chaired by Roy Ash was critical of the Commission's reliance on what were considered piecemeal decision-making procedures. Particular emphasis was directed at the extent to which the Commission focused on individual cases rather than on general policy-making (President's Advisory Council, 1971, p. 27). Another example is contained in a 1973 report issued by the White House Office of Telecommunications Policy (1973). It focused, as did the 1937 Roosevelt Administration report, on the FCC's lack of policy formulation:

> The Commission has published no formal statement of its telecommunications objectives, relying instead on the pronouncement in the (Communications) Act. Whereas it has issued policy statements in a few specific instances it has no telecommunications policy per se. (p. D–34)

In 1974 the Ford administration maintained the tradition of executive criticism on this score by proposing "a long overdue total reexamination" of the FCC and other regulatory agencies (Bacon & Karr, 1974, p. 1).

These examples are characteristic of the conclusions that government studies have produced on the FCC. They indicate the extent to which the Commission has been consistently criticized for what is considered to be the inability to analytically develop goals, turn them into policy formulations, and effectively implement them.

The mountain of criticism from this perspective has not been limited to government analyses. This is particularly evident in a recent book on television station allocations. The authors focus their critical attention in part on what they consider to be a tendency of Commission members to devise criteria for decision-making from a priori rather than analytic grounds. According to them (Cherington, Hirsch, & Brandwein, 1971),

> . . . the FCC, even when it may have recognized the derivative nature of guidelines and specific criteria, either did not clearly trace these derivative elements from what should have been its basic policy objectives—or imperfectly traced them on a priori grounds rather than analytical and statistical grounds. (p. 16)

This argument has been echoed in a 1973 collection of articles edited by Rolla Park of the Rand Corporation. Although the substantive focus of the essays is the Commission's handling of cable television, the major point reiterated throughout is the failure of Commission members to analyze and plan for the broadcasting system. For example, Gary Christensen (see Park, 1973) of the National Cable Television Association argues that "economic research and analysis plays little part in the regulator's decision-making" (p. 15). Douglas Webbink (Park, 1973) writes more cynically based on his years of experience with the Commission's staff:

> . . . it is my impression that those studies had very little effect on FCC decisions. At best, they have affected slightly some of the Commission's opinions on certain questions. . . . In most instances they were probably only used to rationalize decisions that had already been made. At worst, they were ignored when they did not fit the preconceived notion of the Commissioners. (p. 35)

CONCLUSION

The growth of broadcasting in America has certainly been paralleled by the amount of criticism directed at the system. It appears that as the broadcasting system has rapidly become embedded in the complex financial networks of contemporary capitalism,[18] the system's product has quite literally become more and more visible and subject to increasing criticism. However, the visibility of the product does not account for the specific target of much of that criticism—the Federal Communications Commission, one of several so-called "independent" regulatory agencies noted for their lack of visibility. This review of criticism directed at the FCC over the years clearly indicates why I earlier considered comments to the effect that the Commission is generally "under the gun" to be somewhat understated. The Commission has been criticized for most every imaginable reason—to the extent that its alleged performance failures are often linked to quite contradictory influences. Some argue that the Commission fails because it is excessively dependent on such interests as the major commercial broadcasters and the Congress; others contend that the FCC's problems stem from its lack of ties to important sources of support, that is, it is too independent. One cannot help but think at times that the critics must be referring to different organizations.

One obvious source of this difficulty is that analysts too often concentrate on judging the FCC from a particular perspective on how the Commission *should* operate based on the values and interests of an analyst armed with a very selective reading of the Communications Act. For example, it may be that those who see excessive Commission dependence are viewing the agency as failing to optimize its regulatory or control function, whereas those focusing on the Commission's independence do so because they see the Commission as failing to maximize its promotional function (fostering communications development). Though it is no doubt valuable (and sometimes unavoidable) to look at the ways in which the FCC does or does not measure up to a

---

[18]For a brief report on the ties between the broadcasting networks and major financial institutions see Barnet and Muller (1974, p. 235).

desired standard, arguments about what the agency ought to be doing have clouded serious attempts to understand precisely what the Commission *is* doing and *how* it is going about doing it.

Another tendency in analyses frequently compounds the problem: They are based on the explicit assumption that organizations behave in a rational fashion. A typical example of statements that try to provide some theoretical underpinning to the analysis of FCC activity is this one (Noll et al., 1973) in which the primary assumption made is that ". . . the FCC's decisions are the result of rational optimizing behavior. Given the information available to them, the commissioners attempt through their decisions to maximize some objective function" (pp. 120–21). It is, of course, not generally wrong to make such assumptions about rational optimizing behavior; they are particularly common and useful in certain economic analyses of organizations. However, the assumption that the Commission has an explicit objective that it tries fully to attain, actually glosses over what may be an important characteristic of the FCC: it may not operate at all in terms of maximizing specific objectives. Perhaps before discussing what the Commission ought to be doing, one should try to avoid starting from such normative criteria as rational decision-making and optimizing behavior, for avoiding these may provide a key to the actual function of the Commission's work.

To understand this point, let us consider again the mountain of criticism directed at the Commission. By assuming that the Commission should operate in a rational, efficient manner, critics point up the absence of such operation as a problem—but a problem for whom? The Commission's muddled procedures, its "failure" to analyze and plan, indeed all of its alleged shortcomings may very well turn the actual regulation and promotion of the system over to those with the power and resources to act on their own interests. Although there are, of course, important differences between, for example, CBS and NBC (many of which are discussed in subsequent chapters), the nature of the regulatory system may nevertheless assure that it is they who settle differences and not an "ineffective" regulatory commission. In addition to this, the very ineffectiveness of the FCC may be useful in providing an institutional target for those dissatisfied with the system's shortcomings—to the obvious benefit of those with a financial stake in controlling the broadcasting system. Though this process may not operate in all instances, it can illuminate why, despite all of the criticism and the several major technological developments, the basic structure of the broadcasting system and its regulation have remained unchanged over several decades.

The next chapters offer several perspectives that reflect, expand, and challenge both the critical literature and this interpretation of it. They provide conceptual schemes for understanding the Commission's behavior in the four detailed case studies that follow.

3
Four Perspectives

Most analyses of organizations take one or more of the following three perspectives: (1) the organization is viewed as a single entity attempting to get the most of a specific value or set of values; (2) the organization is considered as a set of units, such as particular departments or individual members, in pursuit of what may be incompatible values; and (3) the organization is taken as embedded in a set of organizations attempting to achieve what may be incompatible ends. This chapter considers these and examines a fourth which views organizations as responding to a complex environment with simplifying behavior.

These perspectives, particularly the third and fourth, offer insights into the regulatory history of FM, UHF, CATV, and STV, and help to appraise the Commission's decision-making process and the many proposals made over the years to improve it.

THE ORGANIZATION AS RATIONAL ACTOR

The first approach has carried many labels. I will assess a few of these in order to consider its fundamental characteristics and weigh its usefulness for this analysis.

Allison has characterized this perspective as the "rational-actor" paradigm. He develops it in the context of research on decision-making during the Cuban Missile Crisis. Allison contends that the point of an explanation from this approach is to show how a government or other organizational unit could have chosen to act in a particular way given the problems that it had to face. In other words, if a nation acted in a certain way, it must have had a certain type of goal; the analyst's job is to predict what the focal organization will do or explain what it would have done by calculating the rational course of action given a specific objective (Allison, 1971, p. 5). For the purposes of analysis, the organization is treated as an individual unit attempting to attain fully one or more goals.   Simon (1957) has discussed this approach in terms of what he calls the "means–ends schema," or the application of logically connected tactics to a hierarchy of goals. He contends that to analyze decision-making activity from this perspective is to look upon it fundamentally as the process of choosing from various alternatives those means that are most appropriate for reaching desired ends, recognizing that

> Ends themselves, however, are often merely instrumental to more final objectives. We are thus led to the conception of a series, or hierarchy of ends. Rationality has to do with the construction of means-ends chains of this kind.   (pp. 62–64)

The analyst thus views organizational decision-making as proceeding through a logically connected means–ends chain.

This process of logically applying means to ends has been characterized by Katz and Kahn as "machine theory." They label it in this way because they believe that those who defend its explanatory usefulness argue, at least implicitly, that just as a mechanical device is built with a particular set of specifications for accomplishing a task, an organization is constructed according to a specific blueprint in order to achieve a given purpose. From this perspective, attention is generally concentrated on the division of organizational tasks, the standarization of roles, and the integration of decision-making power (Katz & Kahn, 1965, pp. 71–72).

Steinbruner (1974) has termed this approach the "analytic paradigm" and considers it along with other perspectives in his research on decision-making for the once proposed NATO multilateral nuclear force. Employing the image of the "blueprint" that is often used in discussing this approach, he considers the basic process to be one of decomposing problems into component parts and evoking a deliberate procedure to reach a decision. Of primary importance here is the reduction of possible units to a comparable metric. Thus, the decision-maker seeks an optimal solution under given constraints through direct calculation. Steinbruner considers cost-benefit analysis to be an important recent application of this approach.

In summary, using a rational-actor perspective, the analyst views the organization as an integrated unit structured to attain fully a value or values. This structure is established by translating a specific collection of objectives into a preference set and assessing the consequences of each component of that set. The organization is assumed to be comprised of members who basically agree about the particular ends before it and actively seek out the best possible ways to achieve those ends by rationally assessing the value of every alternative means. This does not mean that differences among members within the organization are entirely ignored—they are simply regarded as less important than the organization's general ends. It is reasoning that is often used by economists who view corporations as profit-maximizing organizations. Although it may be understood that not all members of the organization view this goal as preeminent, the goal can nevertheless be used to explain the decision-making of the organization, if that decision-making conforms to the notion of profit maximization.

How can one apply this perspective to the processes that have characterized FCC decision-making in the cases comprising this analysis? Can one determine a particular value or hierarchy of values that the Commission has generally considered to be desirable and assess the extent to which decision-making has been characterized by a rational assessment of alternatives for attaining that value or set of values? One possibility is to consider the concept of localism. As was pointed out earlier (pp. 19–21), some have considered a localized broadcasting system to be the primary standard of Commission decision-making in this area. One might analyze the extent to which this value has been prominent in decision-making on FM radio, UHF, cable, and subscription television. Specifically, can we, as Allison suggests, "reconstruct" the process of FCC activity to show that the Commission has generally sought to develop stations in as many localities as possible with the control of ownership and programming decentralized to the local level?

The task then is basically to isolate a particular value, such as localism, or a specific set of values, localism and perhaps program diversity, and show that an attempt to maximize their attainment is the most useful way to understand decision-making processes in these cases.

INSIDE THE ORGANIZATION

But what about what happens inside the FCC? Doesn't the rational-actor approach, derived as it is from considering the organization as an integrated unit, lead one to ignore the extent to which individuals within the organization are differentially attached to its goals? Or as Katz and Kahn (1965) note in their critique of "machine theory":

> The concepts paid little attention to the subsystems of organization with their differential dynamics and their own interchange within the organization. Each subsystem in the process of interchange codes and filters its input according to its own characteristics. (p. 73)

The result is to look inside the organization, to consider the ends of subunits, such as particular bureaus, or those of individual members themselves. From this perspective the organization is viewed less monolithically and more as a loose coalition of units trying to attain what may be somewhat different values.

One especially good discussion of this approach is developed by Anthony Downs (1967) in his work *Inside Bureaucracy*. Downs argues that the efficient internal coordination that is often assumed to be a constant in "rational-actor" analyses is in actuality rarely present because the very nature of complex organizations creates many obstacles that prevent spontaneous coordination with some measure of efficiency. Downs views these obstacles as falling into two major categories: technical limitations (e.g., blocks to efficient information flows) and conflicts of interest (e.g., struggles over who actually controls decision-making). He sees the need to reduce such obstacles to manageable levels of difficulty as a primary basis for the growth of elaborate hierarchical authority structures. Hierarchy develops not merely to achieve a particular organizational goal, but more importantly to overcome technical problems and conflicts over power. Derived from his discussion of hierarchical development is a typology of bureaucratic officials that is based on the "nature of the authority position" they come to occupy. For example, he contends that the middle levels of a bureau hierarchy normally contain more of what he calls "conservers," or individuals who seek convenience and security in their positions. These are generally ". . . ex-climbers unable to rise higher, 'natural' conservers at the peaks of their careers, and middle-aged officials who have lost their youthful energy" (p. 99). One way to use this approach for explaining FCC behavior is to consider the differences among officials that stem from their positions along the authority hierarchy. Noll (1971b, pp. 27–28) makes this very point when he claims that the Commission is biased against innovations such as cable and subscription television because of just such a preponderance of middle level "conservers" in its ranks. Hence, one way to use the internal view is to look at differences among organizational members that result from their occupying positions at different levels in the bureaucratic hierarchy.

Another way to understand decision-making processes from the internal view is to consider the different interests that can develop from the vertical instead of the horizontal differentiation of the organization, i.e., from the division of tasks as opposed to the division of authority.

The literature on organizations is replete with statements on the benefits of task specialization. Many classic acronyms such as Luther Gulick's "POSDCORB" have been developed as a means of recalling the "proper" way to attain the "best" form of specialization (Gulick & Urwick, 1945).[1] Recent studies, such as Chandler's (1962) comparative analysis of the development of American business firms have put such acronyms to rest by showing that no optimum mode of specialization is attainable since any form of task division becomes more and more problematic over time. This is true whether such divisions are based on functional or substantive criteria, as well as whether they are tightly coordinated in a centralized structure, such as the Ford Motor Co., or decentralized in a quasimarket divisional arrangement, such as that of General Motors. The primary basis for this assertion is that

[1]POSDCORB refers to planning, organization, staffing, directing, coordinating, reporting, and budgeting.

specialization tends to breed loyalties to a particular task that are often detrimental to the achievement of more general organizational goals. In his work on organizational structures in contemporary China, Schurmann (1971) points to one way of overcoming, or at least managing, this problem: periodically change the basis of the organizational structure from, for example, centralized elite to local mass control, and vice versa. He argues that this can release new energy and thereby prevent ossification. He boldly ventures to claim that a strategy of periodic structural change helps to account for the "success" of such obviously different entities as the People's Republic of China and General Motors (Schurman, 1971, pp. 298–303).

The FCC has undergone two major shifts in its form of vertical specialization that can be traced to problems associated with different types of specialization. Until 1938 the Commission was organized on a divisional basis, with different Commissioners and staff assigned to such distinct functions as broadcasting, common carrier, and mobile services. In 1938 the Commission was reorganized along departmental lines (legal, technical, etc.) in order to permit all Commissioners to take part in decisions involving broadcast regulation and thereby prevent the development of distinct allegiances to particular functions (U.S. *FCC, Annual Report: 1938,* pp. 3–4). Finally, in the early fifties, Congress followed the recommendations of the Hoover Commission and reorganized the FCC once again; this time the FCC returned to a system of functional divisions among bureaus, but with each Commissioner involved with all decisions. The collegial form was thus retained at the Commissioner level and a number of functional bureaus were created. The staff, it was felt, would benefit from service specialization while each Commissioner remained involved in all communications matters. Today the FCC is organized into five bureaus: Common Carrier, Broadcast, Cable Television, Safety and Special Services, and Field Engineering.

In conclusion, another way to use the internal view to understand FCC activity is to consider the impact that the specific type of specialization characterizing the Commission's structure has on its decision-making. For example, is the retention of the collegial structure at the Commissioner level an important factor? Does the lack of specialization here make it particularly difficult for Commissioners to become expert in the potential of specific innovations and therefore predispose them to defer to the staff and/or to outside interests? Has the division of tasks between the staffs of the Broadcast and Cable bureaus influenced the way in which cable television has been treated by the Commission as a whole?

Before turning to a third perspective, it is important to note a similarity between the internal and rational-actor approaches. As has been pointed out, the latter treats the organization as an integrated unit trying to fully attain one or more values. Although the internal approach differs from this in that the organization is not presumed to be an integrated unit but a loose coalition, it does treat the elements of this coalition as rational actors attempting to achieve what may be conflicting standards. This common thread of value-optimization running through these two perspectives is also contained in a third approach that focuses on the organizational context.

OUTSIDE THE ORGANIZATION

Although the above two approaches differ to the extent that attention is directed at internal organizational dimensions, they are also similar in that both focus attention on the organization as the center of explanation. Thus, whether the Commission is treated as rational actor or as a loose coalition of actors, the basis of explanation continues to be the organization itself. Haas and Drabek (1973), among others, consider this to be a significant weakness of these perspectives, particularly for understanding how organizational change takes place. They view these approaches as limited because

> . . . organizations are viewed as existing in a vacuum. External environments, as constraint systems, which might serve as sources of change, are not mentioned. Organizational change is viewed as originating with internal decision-making given stated objectives. External pressures for change exerted at varied levels within the organizations are excluded. (p. 41)

A third approach considers the significance of the relationship between the FCC and organizations in its environment.

It has been only since the 1960s that academic analysts of organizational behavior have explicitly begun to recognize the significance of the organizational context for understanding the activity of a focal organization. Furthermore, the principal focus of many of these analysts has been on the form of technology in the organization's immediate environment. Technology has been considered the chief determinant of the structural characteristics defining the organization and the behavior of its members (cf. Woodward, 1965; Zwerman, 1970). Applying this line of thinking to broadcast regulation, one might look at the influence of technological innovations in the broadcasting market on the structure of the Commission and the behavior of its members. But this is at best an overly simplistic view of organizational processes—one that tends to reify technologies.

Another possibility is to consider the environment not as a form of technology, but as a set of organizations that interact with the one of primary concern. According to this approach, consider the interaction of external organizations with the FCC in comparing processes that have led to specific outcomes.

Such external organizations include other governmental organizations that are concerned with broadcast regulation: the Congress, especially the Commerce Committees in each House; the Executive, recently involved through the White House Office of Telecommunications Policy; the Department of Justice, especially its Antitrust Division; the Courts; the Departments of Defense, Commerce, State, and H.E.W.; and various branches of state and local governments. In addition to these are industry organizations such as the three major broadcasting networks, multiple station owner groups, the National Association of Broadcasters, the Maximum Service Telecasters, and the National Cable Television Association, among others. Other private corporate organizations, such as banks and advertising companies, are not directly part of the broadcasting industry but significantly influence it. Finally, foundations, commissions, and so-called "public interest" groups can also be considered among contextual organizations.

It is important to recognize that the organizational context approach departs from a concern solely for the extent to which a particular organization is constrained, or, in the language that is commonly used to describe the FCC, "captured" by other organizations. For though this view is an especially valuable one, it has its limitations. First, it generally does not deal with the extent to which the focal organization attempts to develop a constituency relationship with organizations in its environment for both technical as well as political support. Thus, is it not equally important to consider the possibility that an organization like the FCC actively seeks out its environment to gain the support necessary to maintain or expand its authority, to protect itself from attempts to abolish it or subordinate it to other agencies, and to secure the budget it wants? A second extension of the organizational constraint model is to take it beyond the emphasis on one type of relationship, that of the organization under analysis and those in its environment, by considering the extent to which relationships *among the latter* influence the focal organization. For example, one might inquire as to the extent to which the relationship between major commercial broadcasters and the House Commerce Committee influences FCC decision-making on broadcasting innovations, in addition to the broadcaster–FCC or Congress–FCC relationships. Emery and Trist (1965, pp. 21–32) have suggested such a perspective in their analysis of an industrial firm that declined rapidly due, they claim, to the failure of company officials to appreciate changing relationships among organizations in the company's environment. Thus, particularly in an environment that is undergoing rapid change and becoming more complex, factors within that environment over which an organization has little control or about which it has little knowledge may interact to cause significant changes in that focal organization.

The organizational context approach, then, expands the basis for understanding decisional processes beyond the boundaries of the organization that formally makes decisions. It suggests looking into the extent to which external constraint is a key element in those processes. It leads us to consider whether and, if so, how the focal organization invests in a potentially supportive environment. Finally, it suggests analyzing the changing relationships among forces comprising that environment.

Each of the three perspectives considered thus far can be viewed as dealing with a different type of constraint upon an organization. From the rational-actor perspective, it is a particular value or set of values that constrains organizational members to behave in a certain way. For example, localism may control the range of activity that FCC members pursue. The internal view points to such factors as conflicts between different bureaus in the organization as constraints on the behavior of its members. Finally, the organizational context approach looks to other organizations as constraining factors. The next section considers a fourth approach that focuses on a constraint not typically considered in analyses of organizational behavior: complexity. The uniqueness of this perspective merits more lengthy consideration.

COMPLEXITY AND THE STATUS QUO

A Critique of Analytic Approaches

Although differences exist between the organizational context approach and the first two approaches described, all three perspectives do share an important element in common: Each assumes that a focal unit attempts to maximize certain goals. Though the set of units is different, that is, a group of organizations as opposed to a single one or parts of one, rational maximization is still assumed to dominate the decision-making process. Considering this latter characteristic, Steinbruner labels approaches such as those that have been considered thus far as "analytic."

He contends that theories based on analytic assumptions are the most frequently used in studies of collective decision-making. Why has this been so? Why has it been that for many years the extent of the changes that have been made in fundamental assumptions about how organizations operate have been variations on an essentially analytical idea? It is not my purpose to detour with a detailed intellectual history of the subject. Such a tangent would lead us to consider classic arguments of Marx or Kuhn's recent formulation, both of which detail the tendency of particular paradigms to remain dominant despite a decline in their ability to explain (Marx & Engels, 1947; Kuhn, 1970). While this is a fascinating area of inquiry, to veer off into it would not be useful for this specific analysis.

Nevertheless, two factors are well worth discussing in order to understand better the next approach to be considered as well as how it might be applied. One important reason why explanations based on the analytic view have maintained their dominant position is suggested by Steinbruner. He contends that the idea of rationality, which is fundamental to analytic perspectives, has all too frequently been linked "in our habits of mind" with the concept of adaptation. The result, according to him, is that

> . . . the only evidence against rationality thus becomes behavior which seems obviously maladaptive. Since adaptation is so closely related to survival itself, maladaptive behavior is *perforce* a rare event. The slowness to challenge rational assumptions in any radical way seems closely related to this association with adaptation.   (p. 50, n. 5)

One of the basic values of his approach is that it suggests how to use the notion of adaptation without connecting it to the concept of rationality.

Another important related point is that it takes more than conjecture about alternative possibilities to create a shift in underlying assumptions. Arrow (1974) has recently suggested that it is a preponderance of "coercive fact" that is in reality "more persuasive than any speculation about potential benefits from change" (p. 52). Since approaches based on the analytic perspective have been so closely linked to the idea of adaptation, it has been difficult to find "coercive facts" to break the tautology that develops from such a link. "Explanations" are often not subject to falsification.

The idea that coercive fact is more important than speculation about alternatives in bringing about change is instructive not only for understanding the lack of change in the general strategies used by organizational actors. It is suggested here, and discussed at greater length later, that a lack of perceived "coercive facts" helps explain why FCC members have not shifted their approach to the broadcasting industry, despite much speculation about alternatives.

The link between rationality and adaptation, as well as the lack of speculation about alternatives, have contributed to the continued significance of approaches based on analytic assumptions.[2] Steinbruner argues, however, that such approaches are increasingly coming under closer scrutiny and may be giving way to alternatives. He claims that this emanates from an increasing concern with the inability of analytically based approaches to prove useful in dealing with complex decision problems.

One important reason why approaches based on analytic assumptions are proving difficult to use is because they assume an infinitely open organizational agenda. In other words, arguments based on the analytic perspective generally take for granted the ability of organizational members to consider all relevant factors. Thus, for example, if FCC members perceived a problem to exist in the broadcasting system, it would be assumed that a comprehensive search for solutions to this problem would be conducted. The analytic view is generally at a loss to deal with the failure to undertake such a search or, more generally, the failure to consider all relevant variables. Arrow (1974) has re-

---

[2]The word "analytic" is used rather than "rational" to avoid associating the alternative to be suggested with "irrational" decisionmaking.

cently referred to this in his discussion of problems associated with what he calls "maximization theory." According to him,

> In classical maximizing theory it is implicit that the values of all relevant variables are at all moments under consideration. All variables are therefore *agenda* of the organization . . . . On the other hand it is a commonplace of everyday observation that the difficulty of arranging that a potential decision variable be recognized as such may be greater than that of choosing a value for it. (p. 47)

One of the important characteristics that is considered in the case studies is the problem that each innovation has had in finding a place on the FCC's agenda.

The organizational agenda is not the only item whose uncertainty is often neglected by analytic approaches. Uncertainty is generally conceived of here in a narrow way. It is typically assumed that an inference structure can be imposed on a decision-making problem with variables that are reducible to a comparable metric. Furthermore, it is generally assumed that the range of possible outcomes is known in advance and that the rules governing the problem area are specifiable and stable. The only matters that are left to the decision-maker are the determination of the particular values to be maximized and the calculation procedure. However, experience with organizations has made it clear that a set of assumptions such as these makes it very difficult to understand many of the problems that people in organizations have to face. As Steinbrunner (1974, p. 18) has noted, the imposition of sufficient structure on a situation so that potential outcomes can be described and their occurence probabilities clearly estimated is itself very much a matter of uncertainty.

The Complex Problem

It is more useful to view the entire process of structuring a complex problem as subject to much uncertainty, rather than to specific guidelines. This is particularly true of the complex problems that typically comprise the work of organizations. Complex problems are those that embody the following characteristics:

1. The central variables of the problem may take a multiplicity of possible values.

2. Problems are embedded in structural uncertainty; i.e., there are major differences between the information available to the organization and its actual environment.

3. Decision-making power is dispersed among several different parties.[3]

Steinbruner argues that because these factors are so often an integral part of

---

[3]This is derived from Steinbruner's formulation. Cf. Steinbruner (1974, p. 18).

the decision-making process, analytically based perspectives provide insufficient grounds for explanation. It is therefore important to consider an approach for understanding how organizational processes develop in response to complexity. One might argue from this perspective, for example, that in certain situations a structure will be imposed on an area of decision-making, not so much because of its usefulness for reaching an optimal solution to a specific problem, but rather in order to resolve the uncertainty of a complex situation. This imposed structure may be rooted in a strong preconceived belief in the kind of outcome that is in some sense proper, or may emanate merely from a long-established technique for simplifying complex problems.

A Response: Simplifying Complexity

These possibilities derive from a consideration of what Steinbruner calls the cybernetic paradigm. More specifically, this section treats that aspect of the paradigm that concerns complex decisional problems—what he calls the "cognitive approach." It is a perspective that is valuable for social scientists because it provides a way to consider organizational beliefs as perhaps other than goals to be achieved in an optimally rational way. For those interested in public policy, it provides a way to consider organizational processes that do not appear to be clearly rational as at least other than deviant and hence to be rejected as unproductive for achieving desired outcomes.

Among the central assumptions of the cognitive approach is the recognition that the information-handling ability of organizations is a scarce commodity. Whereas analytic perspectives assume that organizations can handle almost all relevant material, the cognitive approach helps us recognize that organizations are limited in their ability to search for and process relevant information. This limitation is even more pronounced under the conditions of complexity outlined above. There is thus a cost to the organization for its information-processing activities. To deal with such costs organizational members typically develop a set of rules or codes to govern the way in which information is handled. In other words, they create working assumptions about the areas that are to be considered legitimate sources of relevant information and, in addition, develop procedures for processing it. It is important to recognize, however, that the very process of establishing such a set of assumptions involves costs. As Arrow (1974) has noted: "Drawing up rules to take care of all possible relevant contingencies is itself highly costly in terms of effort and in particular of information, namely, information about the range of possible contingencies and their effects" (p. 74). Thus, there are costs attached not only to the processing of information, but also to the development of rules to expedite such processing. Because of these costs, organizational decision-makers generally limit these activities.

One way to establish limitations is to rely on the set of rules or working assumptions established early in the organization's history. By following long-standing patterns, organizational members avoid the costs of changing the rules of their organization. Arrow specifically points to this in his discussion of the centrality of history for understanding organizational processes in business firms: ". . . history matters. The code is determined in accordance with the best expectations at the time of the firm's creation. Since the code is part of . . . the organization's capital . . . the code of a given organization will be modified only slowly over time" (p. 56). Why is it modified slowly, if at all? Arrow offers an answer in an economic metaphor. He considers the process of code formation a capital accumulation that is irreversible for the organization. According to him: "It follows that organizations, once created, have distinct identities, because the costs of changing the code are those of unanticipated obsolescence" (p. 55). Thus, a first important notion derived from the assumption of a scarcity of information-processing ability is that organizations rely on historically established codes for accomplishing their tasks. These codes help to define not merely the procedures to be used, but also the ways in which problems are perceived and the areas in which solutions are sought.

The last notion leads to a second important insight: Costs attached to the processing of information narrow the search for solutions to perceived problems to the area of established information channels. For, as Arrow notes, it is "cheaper to open certain information channels rather than others in ways connected with these abilities and this knowledge" (p. 41).[4] He cites examples of the explorer in unknown territory who finds it easier to explore areas near to those already covered, of the chemist for whom it is easier to study chemicals of compounds similar to those already analyzed, and of the investment analyst who tends to stay within the same selected list of securities because more information about the same is cheaper than acquiring the initial information about other securities needed to begin analyzing (Arrow, 1974, p. 51). The point is that once one recognizes that there are important costs associated with organizational search, it becomes clearer why decision-makers continue both to perceive problems in certain ways and to concentrate on specific areas for the solution to these problems, even when it becomes apparent that problems should be perceived differently and solutions sought in new areas.

Thus, two major sources of increased costs are linked to a shift in the organizational code; one is derived from the costs of investing in the establishment of a new code and the other from the early absolescence of the original code.

It is at this point that a connection can be made between the idea that organizations rely on historically established codes for extended periods of time

[4]This point has also been made by Cyert and March (1963).

and the three perspectives discussed in previous sections. The rational-actor, internal, and organizational context approaches provide concrete meaning to the general concept of "historically established codes" beyond the somewhat *mechanical* analysis of Arrow. Although it is certainly an insight to view general information processing as a costly investment, it is important to consider other investments that shed further light on why organizations follow historically established patterns. Historical constraints are provided as well by investments in particular values that the members of an organization, in many cases its founders, may have considered desirable. For example, an early investment in the concept of a localized broadcasting system may have constrained the way in which the FCC subsequently dealt with innovations into that system. Similarly a long-established set of internal structural characteristics may have affected the FCC's decision-making on such innovations. Finally, those relations that have developed over time between the Commission and the broadcasting industry can as well be viewed as costly investments that continue to influence Commission activity. The point is that discussing the influence of history does not refer to the impact of a vague, abstract force, but rather to costs attached to very specific decisions that were made and relationships developed during the early years of broadcast regulation.

Here Steinbruner's work becomes instructive. He advances the discussion of why organizations stay within the bounds of historically established patterns by pointing to the results of this for organizations operating within complex environments.

Steinbruner argues that organizations respond to complexity in a number of ways that are difficult to understand within what he calls "analytic assumptions." The following are some of the response patterns that are important for the purposes of this analysis.

1. Organizational members typically respond to complexity by imposing a structure on it rather than by using probabilistic methods of an objective or subjective type. They try to eliminate the uncertainty of variety by developing a set of simplifying rules. According to Steinbruner (1974), the organization "constantly struggles to impose clear, coherent meaning on events, uses categorical rather than probabilistic judgments in doing so, and thus expects to anticipate outcomes exactly rather than have to assign probabilities to a range of outcomes" (p. 112). Thus, a tradeoff appears to be made: Decision-makers gain the ability to act with some consistency in the fact of complexity by closing off new sources of information. They essentially avoid complexity by operating within the confines of a simplified cognitive structure.

2. Organizational actors generally ignore information that does not conform to this cognitive structure. Rather than constantly reevaluating a preference set in the light of new data, they avoid the potential uncertainties that such new

data may bring. Since the control of uncertainty entails a highly focused sensitivity, "most incoming information will be shunted aside, having no effect. This decision-maker is not calculating alternative outcomes and will also not be broadly sensitive to pertinent information" (p. 67).

3. Decision-makers also try to avoid the value conflicts inherent in the complex problem. One example would be the FCC response to the conflict over deciding whether to pursue an innovation such as FM radio at the expense of maintaining the established AM radio system. The response is often a denial that such values are actually in conflict—both can therefore be pursued at the same time.

4. A number of more subtle mechanisms exist that assist organizational actors in the management of complexity. The following are three important ones:

a. *Images and arguments from analogy.* These are well-established notions that have been used to structure similar situations. Steinbruner (1974) uses the example of the so-called "domino theory" in which a chain of events is likened to a set of falling dominoes. According to him, conceptions such as this "provide internal anchors around which inference mechanisms of the mind can structure ambiguous information" (p. 115). He suggests that such conceptions are particularly useful because they have a strength independent of direct evidence that derives from the simplicity of the inference structure which they embody.

b. *Inferences of transformation.* The complexity of competing values is often dealt with by splitting these values into short- and long-run components. Conflicts that might mean the gain of one value at the expense of the other are transformed into equally favorable values within their respective time frames. That is, conflicts are avoided by claiming to pursue one value for the short run, whereas the other is considered to be of long-range significance. This tactic is analyzed later as a common one used by FCC members in responding to innovations into the broadcasting market; FCC decision-makers typically consider innovations not so much in conflict with established media as long-run possibilities to supplement the established system that should remain dominant for the short run.

c. *Inferences of impossibility.* This is a mechanism by which complexity is avoided through the use of negative logic. According to Steinbruner (1974),

> In formal systems of logic, an elaborately constructed argument can be invalidated by the discovery of a single contradiction. Thus, an empirical generalization in mathematics, which might be based upon considerable positive evidence, can be destroyed by a single negative instance. (pp. 117–18)

As applied to organizations, competing claims are avoided by setting up a system whereby one piece of negative evidence can be used to nullify the more novel of the claims.

5. The final set of response patterns consists of modes of thinking that are common within the cognitive perspective. Steinbruner contends that organizational actors adopt characteristic modes of thinking in order to deal with complexity that do not conform to modes expected from actors operating within an analytic framework. The following are examples of two that are relevant to this analysis of the FCC:

a. *Grooved thinking.* This mode provides an organizational member with a way to simplify complex problems by applying long-established techniques to problem solving, even though the context of these problems may have changed significantly and therefore call for the use of new techniques.

b. *Theoretical thinking.* This is also a simplifying mode. However, it involves not the application of established techniques, but rather the imposition of historically developed beliefs to particular problems. Steinbruner considers it one in which decision-makers adopt abstract and extensive belief patterns that are internally consistent, stable over time, and to which a great amount of commitment is directed (Steinbrunner, 1974, p. 131).

In summary, the cognitive perspective provides a way in which to understand how history and complexity affect the operation of organizations. Specifically, it points to how historically established interests and instruments affect, and are used to simplify, the variety of a complex environment. Before considering how useful this perspective is for understanding the FCC's response to innovations in the broadcasting market, let us look at several concluding points.

Two Differences: Cognitive Consistency and Organizational Change

While the approach outlined here is largely dependent on Steinbruner's formulation, it is important to discuss two areas that warrant divergence from his perspective. First, Steinbruner basically views the cognitive perspective as grounded in psychological assumptions. Chief among these is that individuals strive for cognitive consistency; that is, when confronted with a complex environment, decision-makers relieve uncertainty by applying a consistent structure to that environment (Steinbrunner, 1974, pp. 97–100). In the case of the FCC's regulation of broadcasting, he might argue that the Commission has developed a particular conception of what the broadcasting system should be like, not from some rational calculus of priorities or from industry pressure, but in order to relieve the psychological uncertainty of operating in a complex environment. It is not necessary, however, to accept the latter component of his interpretation in considering the general utility of the approach. One can instead argue that the conception of the way in which the broadcasting system should operate is something that has developed from a number of historical realities, the pressures that develop as a result of these, and the need to simplify a complex environment in order to operate upon it, rather than from an assumed psychological need to relieve uncertainty. In addition to this, one can expand the conception of historical influence beyond the narrow bounds described by Arrow to include constraints embodied in the other three perspectives considered thus far. That is, we can regard not only information processing as a costly investment, but also specific values such as localism, particular bureaucratic arrangements, and established relationships with and among other organizations.

A second area in which Steinbruner's analysis falls short is organizational change. One cannot help but get the impression from Steinbrunner's argument that once a particular cognitive structure is developed to simplify a complex environment, there is no basis from which to conceive of the organization changing that structure. Steinbruner's very emphasis on why organizations avoid change makes it all the more difficult to conceive of change actually taking place. Arrow provides a way to deal with change within the basic framework of Steinbruner's approach by considering the significance of "coercive facts." According to Arrow (1974),

> the opportunity benefit, that is, the change in benefits due to a change in action may rise because of a decrease in the return to the present, unexamined action. In plain language, we have a "crisis." In William James' term, a "coercive fact" may be more persuasive than any speculation about potential benefits from change. The sinking of the *Titanic* led to iceberg patrols. (p. 52)

The point is that organizations generally change, not from the development of alternative possibilities, but rather from a perceived crisis situation. Speculation is treated as excess variety to be avoided by decision-makers attempting to deal with a complex environment by imposing a simple cognitive structure on it. It is generally only those "coercive facts" that cannot be ignored that lead them to reevaluate the organization's basic structure. This argument can be applied, for example, to the FCC by considering that one reason why there is an apparent consistency in the processes that have characterized the Commission's response to innovations in the broadcasting market is that FCC decision-makers have perceived few such "coercive facts" or crises that would lead to change, despite considerable speculation about alternatives suggested by proponents of broadcasting innovations.

Policy Relevance

It was noted earlier that the cognitive approach can provide for the policy maker a way to consider organizational processes that do not clearly follow from analytic assumptions to be at least other than deviant and hence to be rejected as unproductive for achieving desired outcomes. This is particularly important because the few statements in the literature on the FCC that implicitly refer to the cognitive approach do so as part of a general criticism of the Commission's failure to abide by the assumptions of the analytic framework. For example, Coase (1970) is critical of the FCC's inability to change, not because of external pressure or internal conflicts, but because as an organization it "must inevitably adopt certain policies and organizational forms which condition its thinking and limit the range of its policies" (pp. 95–96). In a similar way, Borchardt (1970) has criticized the FCC because he believes that although the conflicting values of participants are recognized, Commission membership "ordinarily closes its eyes to the polycentric nature of the conflicts and treats them as separate from each other" (p. 15). Finally, Cary (1967) has noted the tendency of regulatory agencies to fall victim to "channelized thinking" (p. 2).

These statements suggest the empirical relevance of considering the cognitive approach as a basis for making comparisons among decisional processes. However, since they are made from traditional analytic perspectives, they do not provide us with a theoretical alternative. In other words, evidence of a failure to see problems as interconnected or of a failure to think outside of specific channels is treated as a deviation from a particular conception of what constitutes a "correct" decision-making process, rather than as an attribute of an entirely different approach. The value of the cognitive perspective lies not only in its potential to provide an independent theoretical basis for comparing the above criticized processes, but also because it suggests at least the *possibility* that under conditions of structured complexity, such criticism, though perhaps based on sound evidence, may be unproductive for making sound policy. If it is true that organizational pressures lead people to think in narrow terms, and if that narrow thinking is only broadened in crisis situations, then perhaps rather than simply criticizing such a pattern and trying to conform to some analytic ideal, ways must be found for periodically stimulating abrupt changes or crises. Is it too bold to suggest that Western bureaucracies might benefit from periodic Cultural Revolutions?

4

Broadcasting Innovations: Overview and Early History

I have reviewed the mountain of criticism directed at the FCC and presented a number of approaches to analyze the Commission's activities. I now turn to an overview of the case studies and specifically set the cases in the context of the turbulent, early days of broadcasting.

OUTLINE OF THE CASE STUDIES

1. A series of historical developments established AM radio and VHF television as central to the FCC's conception of how the broadcasting system should operate. Particular constraints created by the Commission's relationship to the Congress and major elements of the broadcasting industry, along with the Commission's concern for localism, help to explain how this happened. The FCC has essentially invested its organizational resources in AM and VHF, and any shift away from these areas would involve not only the costs of investing such resources in new areas, but also those derived from the early abandonment of the Commission's initial investment.

2. Furthermore, the amount of work facing FCC members and, more importantly, the uncertainty that characterizes that work, make it even more costly for the Commission to take on the additional job of reassessing its agenda by considering innovations as potential competitors for primacy. In other words, since (a) FCC decision-makers are often too directly involved in the daily routine of administering the ongoing system, (b) they are often not certain about their power to rearrange their agenda, (c) they cannot assess the probability that such a rearrangement would produce a more satisfactory system, and (d) they stand to lose more if an innovation fails than they would gain if it succeeds, the costs of change become even more prohibitive. In short, complexity further limits change.

3. The Commission simplifies or manages this complexity by imposing a basic conception of how the system should operate, derived not from a calculated preference set but from its historically established agenda.

4. FCC members avoid conflicts between competing systems by splitting them up between short-term and long-term possibilities: The established system is viewed as the short term solution, whereas innovations are considered as supplements to the existing system, or potential contributors "in the long run."

5. Speculation about alternative possibilities for the broadcasting system does not carry the weight that severe disruptions in the existing service would carry as an impetus for change. In other words, discussions about the potential benefits of cable or subscription television do not have the impact that a breakdown in the existing system, such as a severe decline in the reception quality of VHF television, would have. Although speculation has flourished, the lack of what were earlier referred to as "coercive facts" has made it all the more difficult for members of the Commission to be open to change.

As a result, AM radio and VHF television continue to dominate the broadcasting system, while the FCC continues to absorb the criticism of those dissatisfied with that system.

THE EARLY YEARS

Before turning to the first case, it is important to consider relevant features of the early history of broadcast regulation. This is by no means meant to be a comprehensive survey, but merely a discussion of factors in the early history of broadcasting that are particularly important to this study.

Government regulation of the broadcasting system began in an attempt to bring order to what was considered by broadcasters themselves to be an increasingly chaotic and intolerable system. The growing confusion developed because different station operators were attempting to use the same spectrum space in the same geographical area and were therefore interfering with one another. In one of the earliest chronicles of this period in broadcasting history, roughly 1920–27, Chase (1942) wrote that

> chaos rode the air waves, pandemonium filled every loud-speaker and the twentieth century Tower of Babel was made in the image of the antenna towers of some thousand broadcasters who, like the Kilkenny cats, were about to eat each other up. (p. 42)

Most of the time spent by Herbert Hoover, then Secretary of Commerce and therefore responsible for radio regulation, was taken up with responding to complaints about technical interference. Typical of the complaints made at the time came as a result of two broadcasts in Washington, D.C. According to Emery (1971), "For three successive Sundays in 1922, two stations in the Capitol City broadcast services from these churches at the same time on the same wavelength. The result was anything but heavenly'' (p. 26). Regulation through the Federal Radio Commission thus began in 1927 in some measure because the nature of the radio spectrum requires the orderly assignment of scarce spectrum space to stations—and station operators' behavior was far from orderly.

Perhaps more importantly, regulation began in an environment characterized by an anxious industry approaching a reluctant government. Hoover himself considered it to be one of those rare situations in which the industry was practically united in its eagerness for government regulation. Addressing the first of several National Radio Conferences in 1922, he noted with surprise that "This is one of the few instances that I know of in this country where . . . all of the people interested are unanimously for an extension of regulatory powers on the part of the government" (cited in Head, 1972, p. 159). This eagerness grew when court decision in 1923 and 1926 severely restricted the regulatory powers of the Secretary of Commerce.[1] These decisions mandated the granting of a station license to every applicant and limited the Secretary's discretionary authority solely to the selection of a wave length. As a result, the possibility for bringing order to the chaos of the air waves under the existing regulatory system practically disappeared.

This was changed somewhat with passage of the 1927 Radio Act that vested discretionary authority to assign frequencies to the Federal Radio Commission. It is important to understand that the Act simply sought to promote the orderly development of the radio industry by protecting the system from the chaotic interference that characterized broadcasting's early days. It was not to be an instrument of complete state control over the broadcasting system: There was to be no planned program for assigning stations to communities, nor would there be controls on the interconnection of stations into networks. Such actions, it was felt, would entail excessive government interference into a system intended to be governed by free market competition. Remember that this was three years after the Federal Trade Commission (1924) issued a report that criticized the radio industry for monopoly practices.

Why was this stance taken at a crucial time in the development of the broadcasting system? One thing appears certain—the American approach was not based on a foreign precedent. In 1923 the British government created the BBC and thereby asserted direct state control over radio broadcasting.[2]

Perhaps Secretary Hoover should not have been so surprised that the industry would turn to the government and plead for regulation. Some measure of state regulation of private enterprise had been very much a part of the American scene since at least the Interstate Commerce Act of 1887. Such regulation was often sought by major companies and benefited them considerably.

[1]*Hoover, Secretary of Commerce v. Intercity Radio Co., Inc.*, 286 F. 1003 at 1007 (1923) and *U.S. v. Zenith Radio Corp.*, 12 F. (2d) 614 at 618 (1926).
[2]For a good analysis of the development of broadcasting in Great Britain, see Briggs (1961).

Moreover, with the Transportation Act of 1920 came a particular form of regulation that directly established a pattern for the type of government involvement that would guide the broadcasting system: It was the first of a series of laws that sought to protect against competition rather than monopoly by vesting rather vague powers in an independent agency (Noll, 1971b, pp. 37–38).

The Federal Radio Commission, through the 1927 Radio Act, and the FCC, through the 1934 Communications Act, were both charged with the task of regulating the broadcasting system "in the public interest, convenience and necessity." They were both part of this turn toward the protection of major industry interests from what were considered the harmful effects of competition.[3] For whatever reasons—whether because of a desire to protect established private interests, a distrust of the political system, a faith in expert judgments, a Congressional effort to control new industry without having to get involved in its daily business—this new legal structure solidified the hold of RCA on the radio industry and eventually led to what were considered significant problems.

First, since stations were free to develop anywhere there was available spectrum space, they tended to concentrate in areas of high population density where advertising revenues would be greatest. As a result, many communities, particularly those located in rural areas, had no radio service at all. The FCC viewed this development with alarm in its 1938 *Annual Report* in which it reported that 8.1% of the total population and 38.5% of the total land area of the United States were out of the "good-service area of any standard broadcast station" for daytime service, and that for nighttime listening the figures increased to 17.4 and 56.9%, respectively (U.S., FCC, *Annual Report: 1938,* p. 50 and App. f). In 1939 the Commission once again discussed the problem and considered "the economic factors arising from the distribution of the population" to be the major force perpetuating the problem of poor service distribution (U.S., FCC, *Annual Report: 1939,* p. 36).

A second development was also derived, at least in part, from minimal state involvement in regulation. This was the growing control of stations by a few major interests, particularly the three networks, NBC's Red and Blue and CBS. In the late 1930s the FCC began what it called a study of "chain broadcasting" and expressed concern that "As of the end of 1938, less than 3 percent of the nation's total nighttime broadcasting power was utilized by stations not affiliated with one or the other of these three network companies (U.S., FCC, *Annual Report: 1941,* p. 22).

Both a concern for the lack of rural service and the increasing control by the networks led to a more active regulatory role at the Commission. What was significant, beyond its increased activity, was the channel into which that activity was focused. Although the Commission did not consider it possible to

[3]For a further discussion of this point see Holt (1967, pp. 15–19).

restructure an industry that it had helped to promote and into which the American people had invested millions of dollars, it could make certain that these problems would not be repeated with new media sources. Consequently, for example, in the case of FM radio, the FCC not only developed a plan of station assignments, but it also limited the power of individual stations in particular markets. Rather than develop as an independent force in radio, FM would be subjected to controls that actually emanated from the Commission's free market policy toward AM. A similar pattern is explored in the UHF, CATV, and STV cases.

Thus, rather than attempt to *solve* the broadcasting system's problems through the promotion of innovations into that system, the FCC simply attempted to ensure that these innovations would not develop similar perceived problems. In other words, rather than *use* innovations as correctives to expressed problems, the Commission largely sought to control them. The result: an exacerbation of those problems. FM radio was the first to suffer.

5

FM: Radio's Second Chance

> Given the facts presented in earlier chapters,
> only a miracle, one might say, could save us
> from the projection of present trends into an
> indefinite future. But a miracle *has* happened.
> Radio has a second chance.
>
> CHARLES SIEPMANN, (1946, p. 238)

INTRODUCTION

Siepmann's miracle was frequency modulation (FM) radio. He was among
many who claimed (and hoped) that this new use of the radio band would
revolutionize broadcasting in the United States (cf. *Fortune*, October, 1939;
MacLaurin, 1949).

Most of the sparse literature on this subject has dealt with why this revolution failed to materialize. Some have argued that the major influence on the
Commission in its FM rulings has been a concern for protecting major AM
broadcasters such as RCA and CBS. For example, according to Krasnow and
Longley (1973),

> The FCC was able to prevail largely because its policies favored powerful, well-
> established broadcasting interests pushing the development of postwar television. The de-
> velopment of FM broadcasting posed a triple threat—to the dominance of established AM
> stations and networks; to RCA's hopes for quick postwar development of TV and to
> RCA's patents. (p. 92)

Edelman (1950) has essentially echoed this point in his report on radio licensing practices from 1927 to 1947. He concludes that a "fundamental reason for
FM's slow growth has been the opposition of standard broadcast licensees and
other vested interests who stand to lose financially by the establishment of a

new system of broadcasting'' (p. 123). Cf. Siepmann (1946, p. 246), Lessing (1969, p. 269), and Sterling (1971, pp. 181–94).[1]

The major FCC ruling that dealt a severe blow to the FM service was the decision to shift FM from the spectrum area originally assigned to it to an entirely different spectrum location. Barnouw (1968, p. 242) claims that this decision alone made obsolete 500,000 prewar FM receivers and estimates that it cost station owners $75 million to convert transmitters to the new spectrum area. Such high conversion costs were prohibitive for many FM station owners and forced them to sell out their interests to large AM commercial broadcasters, thereby limiting FM's potential to provide an alternative to standard AM fare. This chapter examines how this and other decisions turned radio's second chance into a secondary service.

GETTING ON THE AGENDA

To understand this case it is important to consider the historical context into which FM was introduced. Two factors noted in the previous chapter are particularly significant here: In the 1930s the Commission became increasingly concerned about the concentration of radio stations in urban areas and the centralization of broadcasting power in the major networks. A context characterized by these problems would lead one to expect that the Commission would have been most receptive to FM, since this service promised new networks that would stimulate competition and add service to rural residents. However, the FCC proved to be less than open to FM. It is important to note that one factor in the decisional processes in this case, as well as in the others, is the problem that innovations such as FM radio have had in getting on the Commission's agenda of major broadcasting concerns.

The FM service was developed in the 1930s by Edwin Armstrong, one of broadcasting's technical pioneers.[2] In 1933 he conducted laboratory tests at RCA and a year later performed a crucial test from atop the Empire State Building. He later reported (U.S. Congress, House, 1948) that ''the success of the test surprised even myself'' (p. 6). Armstrong next turned to the prestigious Institute of Radio Engineers, at whose 1935 meeting he demonstrated his new radio technique (Armstrong, 1936), claiming that ''. . . the conclusion is inescapable that it is technically possible to furnish a broadcast service over the primary areas of the stations of the present-day broadcast system which is very greatly superior to that now rendered by these stations.'' The In-

---

[1]This position was reiterated to me in December 1974 in an interview with Henry Geller, at that time a communications specialist with the Rand Corporation.

[2]For an excellent, sympathetic account of Armstrong's work see Lessing (1969).

stitute greeted Armstrong's presentation with near unanimous approval, but the FCC took little note of FM until late in the decade.

Among those who did not enthusiastically respond to Armstrong's demonstration was the FCC's assistant chief engineer who publicly minimized the possibility of developing an FM service because he felt it was a "visionary development" and essentially impractical for current consideration (U.S. Congress, House, 1948, p. 8). As a result of this judgment Armstrong was denied a station construction permit. The Commission's *Annual Report* of 1937 contains a section on "Technical Developments in the Broadcast Art" dealing with both television and facsimile reproduction, but no mention is made of FM radio (U.S. FCC, *Annual Report: 1937,* pp. 27, 44).

By 1938 commissioners began to recognize that Armstrong and his followers might be right. In its *Report* of that year the FCC noted several major advantages that FM could offer broadcasting over the AM service:

1. a material gain in the effectiveness of reception through static, especially the type of static resulting from nearby thunderstorms and from some types of man-made electrical disturbances;
2. the signal-to-noise ratio necessary for satisfactory reception is considerably less than that required for the same reception with a broadcast system employing amplitude modulation;
3. good reception at a greater distance from the transmitter and a correspondingly larger service area for the same power used at the transmitter. (p. 66)

Nevertheless, despite this recognition of FM's technical superiority over the AM service, and despite the Commission's expressed need for an improved radio system that could offer alternatives to AM network control and more extensive rural service, the Commission did not begin to authorize FM commercial development until 1940.

Why did it take so long for the Commission to consider FM radio seriously? Certainly, one important factor was the technical uniqueness of the FM concept. Indeed, Brinton (1962, p. 102) claims that FM contradicted some of the basic rules and constraints that radio engineers and broadcasters had abided by since 1900, and which the FCC had simply taken for granted. Though this may be somewhat overstated, it is accurate to say that few had considered the transmission of signals through frequency modulation to be a feasible possibility. This is primarily because FM was considered a development that could only work, if at all, in the so-called ultrahigh frequency part of the radio spectrum—an area that many felt would require several very costly advances in transmission and reception technology before it could be used (U.S. Congress, House, 1948, pp. 8ff.).

The amount of work that the Commission was required to perform simply to regulate the existing broadcasting system compounded the difficulty of spending time on assessing the value of an innovation into that system. The Commission simply did not have the resources at hand to carry out the work stipulated by the Communications Act. The Commission itself began to complain rather vociferously about this problem in the late 1930s (U.S. FCC, *Annual Report: 1938*). For example, it argued that:

> The administrative task throughout the range of the Commission's functions is large, varied, and difficult. Experience has demonstrated that the Commission is gravely understaffed for its task and that this condition is largely responsible for the accumulation of work and the inability to keep a great part of the work current. Overtime work by the staff is unavoidable and excessive. (p. vi)

This was reiterated in two different sections of the Commission's 1939 *Report* (pp. 6, 89).

In the face of this new development in radio, and with minimal resources of its own, the Commission began to rely on the established industry for guidance and, in particular, on work being done at RCA. In later Congressional hearings on FM it was noted that commissioners and, perhaps more importantly, its engineer in charge of broadcasting depended almost entirely on RCA for technical data on FM (U.S. Congress, Senate, 1948b, p. 164; cf. U.S. FCC, *Annual Report: 1937,* p. 11).

The Commission thereby conformed to a pattern all too common to it and other organizations: In the face of a task that was complex both in terms of the amount of work at hand and technical difficulty, it searched for a solution almost solely within established channels. Although it is, of course, impossible to determine this with certainty, it would probably have been much easier for FM to be considered legitimate in the view of Commission members had it been proposed by RCA's David Sarnoff rather than by a maverick like Edwin Armstrong.

Why was it that Sarnoff did not promote FM radio? RCA had an important stake in the maintenance of the established AM system: It controlled two very profitable radio networks (the Red and Blue); it had major investments in station transmitters and receivers that might be hurt by any significant shift to FM, and it wanted the FCC to reserve large amounts of spectrum space for the development of a television system. Only ten days after Armstrong made public his progress on an FM system at the 1935 Institute of Radio Engineers meeting, Sarnoff announced that RCA was ready to commit itself to the rapid development of an electronic television system with a $1 million initial expenditure (Lessing, 1969, p. 224). One year later, Sarnoff appeared before the Commission to report on "The Future of Radio" and made no mention of FM despite research conducted by RCA engineers that upheld Armstrong's technical expectations (U.S. Congress, House, 1948, pp. 9–10). Although there does not appear to be evidence of direct pressure on the part of RCA to keep FM out of the Commission's view, it is clear that RCA did nothing to promote FM in its early years. Since the FCC had established its most important information-seeking channels directly with RCA, the simple lack of support lessened the chances for quick commercial development of FM.

This example indicates why it is important to consider problematic the very process by which organizational decision-makers create an agenda. If one assumed that all relevant variables are considered in the process of searching for solutions to stated problems, then one would expect FM to have been very much a part of the Commission's agenda of possible solutions. That it was not is largely due to the complexity of the Commission's work and its dependence on established interests for information and advice.

THE RISE OF AN ANCILLARY SERVICE

Even when brought to the FCC's attention, FM was treated as a service that could only be secondary to the established system. At first this does not appear to correspond to the view of FM contained in the Commission's 1940 report (U.S. FCC, *Annual Report: 1940*) accompanying its authorization of FM commercial development:

> Frequency modulation is highly developed. It is ready to move forward on a broad scale and on a full commercial basis. On this point there is complete agreement amongst the engineers of both the manufacturing and the broadcasting industries. A substantial demand for FM transmitting stations for full operation exists today. A comparable public demand for receiving sets is predicted. (p. 66)

At this time the FCC assigned 35 channels to FM in the 43–58 MHz range—enough spectrum space for from 1500 to 2000 stations in the United States.

It is important to understand, however, that this optimism was tempered by a concern to make certain that FM remain in a supplementary position relative to the established broadcasting system. This concern was expressed in another FCC statement on FM (U.S., FCC, 1940). Here it was to be clearly understood that this ". . . new and additional service would not supplant the service of standard broadcast stations generally" (Docket 5805). Furthermore, the FCC (U.S. FCC, *Annual Report: 1940*) tried to make certain that the problem of monopoly, considered by the Commission to be a severe detriment to program diversity in the AM service, would not be repeated with FM. Hence: "to obviate possible monopoly, and to encourage local initiative, no person or group is permitted to control more than one FM station in the same area, and not more than six in the nation as a whole" (p. 68).

This is an example of how the FCC, even at the time of its greatest enthusiasm for FM, focused on avoiding a repetition of what were considered problems with the AM system instead of on using FM to solve them. With localism thwarted by the AM network system, the Commission sought to foster it with the FM service. Yet, by supporting competition within the FM industry, the Commission lost an opportunity to use the service to provide a competitive challenge to the AM system.

As for AM radio's own problems, the Commission searched for solutions from within that service. For example, the FCC's 1941 *Report on Chain Broadcasting* proposed dealing with the problem of monopoly by severing one network from the control of RCA's subsidiary the National Broadcasting Company. Nowhere in the *Report* is the possibility of using the FM service to deal with the problem discussed, despite the Commission's earlier touting of FM's almost static-free signal and superior reception at greater distances than could be received over AM radio. This action appears to stem from the Commission's tendency to associate major solutions with the established broadcasting service, not so much because it succumbed to pressure from the industry—the FCC received no industry pressure to break up NBC—but because its investment in what it called "standard broadcasting" led it both to view that system as primary and to search for solutions within its vicinity.

Another example of the FCC restricting its search to the area of the established interests concerns its position on so-called "clear channel" radio stations. These are very powerful AM stations whose frequency is not shared by any other station within a wide geographical area, thereby allowing these stations very extensive nighttime coverage. The Commission (U.S. FCC, *Annual Report: 1946*) spent a great amount of time attempting to develop a sufficient number of clear channel stations to, as it claimed, ". . . provide standard broadcast service to some 21,000,000 Americans who are not now being satisfactorily served" (p. viii). Once again the Commission looked for solutions to its problems with the AM service within that same service.

This pattern of considering FM as secondary to the established service did not change in 1945, the year that marked perhaps the most significant decision-making on FM. Two decisions were of central importance. First, in June of 1945 the Commission shifted the spectrum assignment of FM radio from its 1940 allocation area around 50 MHz to that around 100 MHz. Second, in August of that same year it approved what was called the "single market plan." This lowered the maximum allowable transmitter power of FM stations in major urban areas and thereby severely hampered attempts to develop an FM network system.

The context of these decisions was one characterized by severe complexity both in terms of the amount of work and its technical difficulty. Despite the wartime "freeze" on FM development, there were, by 1944, 47 stations in operation, 500,000 sets in use and 400 applicants seeking station licenses (U.S. FCC, *Annual Report: 1944*, p. 16; *Annual Report: 1945*, p. 20). In the Commission's 1944 FM hearings, 6000 pages of testimony were received, 650 formal exhibits were presented, and 230 witnesses were heard (U.S., Congress, House, 1948, p. 182). In addition, many claims were made by several different parties for spectrum space following general wartime freezes.

Along with FM proponents, television, safety service, and AM radio interests played a significant role in disputes over spectrum allocations. There simply was not enough spectrum space available to meet everyone's expressed needs and consequently conflicts were inevitable.

THE SPECTRUM SHIFT

The Commission ultimately decided to shift FM radio from its original spectrum allocation. This took place despite opposition not only from such expected quarters as manufacturers of FM equipment and FM station owners, but also from the Commission's own panel of industry experts (the Radio Technical Planning Board) and RCA.

The Radio Technical Planning Board (RTPB) was organized in September, 1943 at the request of the FCC Chairman (U.S. Congress, House, 1948) so that the Commission ". . . might have available the coordinated views of industry respecting radio allocations to the various services" (pp. 215–16). The RTPB was organized by nine industry associations including the Institute of Radio Engineers, the National Association of Broadcasters, and FM Broadcasters, Inc. Dr. W.R.G. Baker of General Electric chaired the Board. Here again, with meager technical expertise of its own, the Commission turned to the industry to plan for future spectrum allocations.

The RTPB panel charged with making recommendations for FM radio primarily addressed the question of whether potential interference might require the shifting of FM from the spectrum area assigned to it in 1940. This concern was raised in November, 1940 by K.A. Norton, a former FCC engineer, who recommended that FM be shifted in order to avoid what he considered to be a serious potential interference problem in the 50 MHz range (U.S. Congress, House, 1948, pp. 88–89). Contrary to Norton's recommendation, the RTPB panel on FM radio held (U.S. FCC, 1945a), by a vote of 19 to 4, that there was ". . . no technical evidence to indicate that certain erratic propagation characteristics of the spectrum would be improved by any shift in the present allocation" (Docket 6651). Instead, the panel proposed that the existing FM band be considerably expanded to permit 75 commercial channels in the 41–56 MHz range "so assigned that they shall be continuous with and include the present FM band" (Docket 6651). This point is significant because it would have ruled out the necessity of converting FM equipment. The panel's position was supported by the RTPB group on General Spectrum Allocations and the recommendation was sent to the Commission (U.S. Congress, House, 1948, p. 88).

RCA was among the major interests that did not support shifting FM to a new spectrum area. It made this position explicit on at least three separate occasions: early in 1945, when two people from the research divisions of

RCA and NBC argued before the Commission that FM should not be moved (U.S., FCC, Docket 6641, March 12, 1945, pp. 130–1); RCA representatives also petitioned against the shift before the Commission in two separate briefs that essentially supported the RTPB position (U.S. Congress, House, 1948, pp. 250–51). On the other hand, CBS supported moving FM to a different spectrum area (Lessing, 1969, p. 258).

What was the basis for the conflicting positions taken by RCA and CBS? One possibility is that the conflict was closely connected to the struggle between RCA and CBS over the specific form that television would take. RCA may have opposed the FM shift because the company was concerned that such an action might set a precedent for shifting television out of its original VHF area and into the ultrahigh frequency region. This would obviously hurt RCA's heavy initial investment in VHF television. On the other hand, CBS may have wanted FM moved because moving television to UHF would have put that company, which had not invested in VHF television, on an equal footing with RCA.[3]

This conflict points to important considerations that have not been addressed in other reports on this case. First, it indicates the extent to which broadcasting problems are tightly interconnected. To claim that FM was hurt solely because of the power of television interests is to gloss over the fact that there were different possible outcomes tied to different industry interests. The evidence suggests that, perhaps because of this, there was no unified broadcast industry interest pressuring the FCC to restrict FM. It is true that CBS tried to curtail FM, and it is also correct to say that RCA did not attempt to directly promote the new service, particularly prior to 1940. However, perhaps because maintaining the status quo in FM meant protecting its television investment, RCA opposed CBS and was at least implicitly aligned with FM supporters on this issue.

The Commission began to turn against the recommendations of its industry panel in 1945. In a report (*Broadcasting,* January 16, 1945) on FM issued early in that year the Commission expressed concern that ". . . 'sporadic E' and 'F2 layer' interference would plague FM in the next few years at its present frequency as the sunspot maximum is approached" (p. 17). In its final report on FM released in June, 1945, the FCC brushed aside claims that any interference, if occurring at all, would be limited to rural areas. The Commission (see *Broadcasting,* July 2, 1945) held firm to the position that ". . . urban as well as rural service will be subject to substantial interference on the lower frequencies" (pp. 64, 68). These technical considerations were the primary stated grounds for shifting FM to the 100 MHz region. Reflecting back on this decision at a 1948 Congressional hearing (U.S. Congress, House,

[3]Support for this interpretation can be found in Lessing (1969, pp. 257–58) and *Business Week* (November 4, 1944, p. 88).

1948), Commissioner George Sterling reiterated the opinion of the Commission majority that it was "in order to avoid interference from sporadic E and F2 reflections that the Commission decided that FM broadcasting should be assigned to the 100 megacycle region" (p. 186).

Although it is difficult to determine precisely why a particular decision is taken by an organization, this is the only reason that FCC members have offered to explain the action. However, a major problem with the explanation is that only one expert witness argued in favor of this position. Following K.A. Norton's appearance before the Commission to testify in favor of the FM shift, seven experts in radio wave propagation contradicted his claims, generally arguing that FM should remain in its originally allocated position (U.S. Congress, House, 1948, pp. 90–95, 125–33). In addition, although the final FM decision was supposed to await completion of atmospheric testing in the summer of 1945, the decision was reached before these tests could be conducted. It is interesting to consider the Commission's interpretation of this development (U.S. FCC, *Annual Report: 1945*):

> Since the Commission desired to have as much information as possible before it prior to making a decision about the FM band, the Commission announced on May 25 that it would withhold the allocation of FM pending further propagation measurements to be made during the summer of 1945. Subsequently, however, the War Production Board advised the Commission that the manufacture of FM, AM, and television transmitters and receivers might begin at an earlier date than was originally indicated to the Commission. . . . Accordingly, the Commission on June 5, 1945, ordered a further argument and hearing in order that a final decision might be reached at the earliest possible date. (p. 20)

The tests considered crucial to determining whether FM was to be moved were thus cancelled, and without any additional testing FM was shifted to a new spectrum area in the 100 MHz range.

There are other factors that make this explanation based on technical considerations a particularly difficult one to comprehend. The space out of which the Commission moved FM was subsequently turned over to television use. Might not television be subject to greater interference problems than the FM service? It was claimed that this was understood by the Commission, but that such interference would do no permanent harm since television would also soon be moved out of this spectrum area (U.S. Congress, House, 1948, p. 190). Though the television service was, in fact, moved out of the area formerly occupied by FM, the space was finally assigned to safety and emergency services (i.e., police, fire, etc.) in the late 1940s.[4] Again, how can emergency services more appropriately occupy spectrum that was considered technically unsuited to an essentially leisure service due to interference prob-

---

[4]While television was moved out of the 50 MHz range, it was never completely moved to the UHF area where the Commission expected to assign it. This development is explored in the next case.

lems? Commissioner Sterling (U.S. Congress, House, 1948) offered this response:

> . . . the Commission recognized, too, that police operations in the 44–50 megacycle region would be subject to interference. . . . operations such as police and fire communications are conducted on an intermittent basis. This in itself diminishes the possibility of encountering serious interference. Moreover, police and fire department messages, for example, that may not go through because of interference can be repeated many times within a relatively short interval of time. Because of this possibility of repeating messages the problem of interference is further minimized. (p. 190)

Although the intermittent nature of such communications and the ability to repeat them cannot be denied, it still appears strange for the Commission to uproot an entertainment medium at great cost to station operators, equipment producers, and receiver owners because of a potential interference problem and subsequently turn over the spectrum space to emergency services that require rapid responses by all concerned.

To understand this decision it is necessary to consider factors other than the technical ones. A concern for localism is of only slight significance here. In its final FM spectrum shift report, the Commission makes brief reference (*Broadcasting*, July 2, 1945) to the need to locate FM in a totally interference free spectrum area because ". . . this Commission, moreover, is under a statutory duty to make available to all people of the United States an efficient nationwide radio service," (p. 64). Although there certainly were forces within the industry opposed to the development of FM, divisions among these interests lessened the strength of the opposition.

An interesting consideration internal to the Commission was considered by Jansky (U.S. Congress, House, 1948). As he testified at 1948 Congressional hearings:

> I have never been able to understand why the Commission undertook to prepare a technical case with its own witnesses against the recommendations of the radio industry.
>
> Having done this, it may have seemed logical to it to accept the finding of its own expert (K.A. Norton) as against the findings of others. Either this is the explanation or the subject was approached with a closed mind. (p. 120)

Although Jansky may well have been pointing to a contributing factor, his argument loses some of its plausibility when it is understood that Norton was no longer working for the Commission. He had spent the last few years working as an engineer in the Army.

Perhaps the last part of his statement warrants more than the passing attention that Jansky gave it. It may very well be that decision-making on FM was approached by Commissioners and staff with a closed mind. Recalling that minds had to be open to a tremendous amount of work, including the determination of how to deal with the burgeoning television and special service industries, it is understandable that an innovation into the radio industry might be viewed solely as an adjunct to the established, or what the Commission called the "standard," broadcasting system. It is of further interest to note that when, three years after the decision, Commissioner Sterling recognized the "error of prediction on the part of Norton," he considered the "complexity of the subject matter involved" to be a major reason for the mistake (U.S. Congress, House, 1948, pp. 191–92).

The consideration of complexity is relevant here, for two further aspects of this decision are related to it. First, the contention that unless FM was shifted it would be hampered is an example of the concept of the "inference of impossibility" discussed earlier (p. 41); that is, when organizational decision-makers become committed to a particular perspective, one piece of evidence against a contrary view is enough for them to reject that view. In the FM case, all but one of the expert witnesses before the Commission denied that interference would pose a problem. Nevertheless, the Commission did shift FM, based on the testimony of one witness. Perhaps since the Commission had consistently viewed FM as ancillary to the established system, it only took one piece of testimony in support of the shift to justify the decision.

The decision to shift FM contains another interesting characteristic of bureaucratic response patterns—the short-run/long-run split. As was noted earlier (p. 41), when faced with contradictory alternatives, organizations tend to deny the contradictions rather than directly recognize them. One method of denial is to split the alternatives into short- and long-term components. Thus, for the short-term, the Commission recognized that there would be problems with uprooting the FM industry and giving its spectrum space to television, but this would actually, it claimed, be of "long-run" benefit to the FM service. In its shift order the Commission stated (*Broadcasting,* July 2, 1945) that it had ". . . a duty to consider the long range effects of its action as well as the effects during the months immediately ahead, and it does not propose to provide an inferior FM service during the decades to come merely because of the transitory advantages which may be urged for an inferior service" (p. 68). In an interview conducted after release of the order (*Broadcasting,* July 2, 1945), Commissioner Jett claimed that although the area around 50 MHz was best for the short-term needs of FM the new area was chosen out of "long-term planning" considerations (p. 13).

Though no specification was made about what these long-term considerations actually were, *Broadcasting* magazine was quick to size up the immediate impact: The FM industry would be severely hurt as existing receivers and transmitters were made obsolete; FM would continue to suffer until producers were able to retool and turn out new highband receivers (*Broadcasting,* November 12, 1945, April 1, 1946). Aside from the harm done to the industry, consider the impact on the owners of the approximately 500,000 FM receivers in use prior to 1945. For these people the Commission could only offer this consolation (*Broadcasting,* July 2, 1945): "Most of these receivers are combination AM–FM and the AM part of the receiver will still continue to be used" (p. 68).

This decision shows that a system that gives legal authority to an agency to make major decisions about resource allocations, but that fails to provide the support for the agency to do a thorough and independent job is essentially inviting conservative decision-making. This form of decision-making hurts innovations like FM, which are treated as challengers to an already viable system.

THE SINGLE MARKET PLAN

A second FCC decision in 1945 continued this pattern. The so-called "single market plan" essentially set maximum limits on the power (20 KW of radiated power) and antenna heights (no higher than 500 feet) of northeast metropolitan stations (Warner, 1948, p. 600). The impact on major FM stations was considerable: The primary station of the chief FM chain, the Yankee network, had its power cut by one-third (Lessing, 1969, pp. 259–60). It has been estimated that the average high-power FM station had its coverage reduced from 150 to 45 miles, thereby curtailing initial attempts to develop a distinct FM network broadcast service (Lessing, 1949, p. 127).

Why was this done? According to Commissioner Sterling (U.S. Congress, House, 1948) the decision was made to prevent monopoly concentration in the FM industry. He contended that:

> To permit higher powered FM stations in the highly congested portions in the United States would, of course, greatly reduce the number of assignments that could be made in such areas and would thus tend to foster monopoly in FM broadcasting. The Commission's allocation policies are designed to permit a large number of FM stations to be authorized so that a maximum number of cities and communities may have their own FM stations. (p. 197)

The argument on behalf of localism appears to be clearer in this decision than in the spectrum shift ruling; that is, license the maximum number of stations in as many locations as possible, even if that requires strict limits on the power of individual stations. Like the spectrum shift decision, this one was characterized by a split among major industry organizations: It was proposed by CBS and opposed by RCA (U.S. FCC, Docket 6768, pp. 29–33). It is difficult to discern precisely the basis of this difference. Perhaps CBS, still lagging behind RCA, might have wanted to prevent the establishment of high-powered stations against which RCA might more easily compete. RCA may have been interested in these stations as future sources of investment.

This decision does appear to be a good example of dealing with complex situations through compartmentalization. Commission decision-makers did not view the radio service as a totality, with FM providing the means to deal with problems in the AM service, such as that of network monopoly. Rather, they separated the services, looking for solutions to the problems of AM radio only in the AM area, while seeking to prevent a repetition of these problems in the FM service. The result was that, although the single market plan might have protected against the development of monopoly in the FM industry, the plan would also help to preserve what the Commission had considered to be a major problem: the concentration of power in the AM radio industry.

MAINTAINING AN ANCILLARY SERVICE

This practice of treating FM as a secondary service continued in the years following these two decisions.

1. AM Control and Program Duplication

The FCC encouraged AM station owners to take over FM operations and duplicate their programming on these stations. In 1945 the FCC gave AM stations permission to do this, while at the same time ruling that FM owners would not be allowed to control more than six FM stations in the nation and only one in a community. The Commission also suspended the new chain broadcasting rules for AM owners of FM stations, including those rules applying to the allocation of option time for network affiliates (Warner, 1948, p. 603).

A 1947 Commission report (U.S. FCC, *Annual Report: 1947*) contains a further explicit example of this position:

> As of March 1, 1947, three-fourths of all FM applications were from standard broadcast (AM) interests and one-third were from newspapers, 23 percent of which were in the standard broadcast field. *These groups are in a position to support the new industry until it reaches profitability.* Standard broadcasters have an advantage in being permitted, thus far, to transmit their programs over FM facilities. (pp. 20–21) (emphasis mine)

By 1950 over 80% of FM station authorizations were in the hands of AM licensess broadcasting in the same geographical area (U.S. FCC, *Annual Report: 1950*, p. 117).

This policy would appear to be particularly detrimental to FM network and independent stations. For with FM shows thrown in free with AM network broadcasts, FM networks and independent stations would have a very difficult time trying to convince advertisers (or anyone else) to pay for FM programming. On the other hand, some have accepted the Commission's view that FM would grow by encouraging AM station owners to purchase FM stations and duplicate their programming on them. Not surprisingly, Charles Jolliffe, while executive Vice President in charge of RCA Labs, claimed before a Congressional committee (U.S. Congress, House, 1948, p. 246) investigating FM in 1948 that such a policy "means so much to the advancement of FM" that it was essential to retain it.[5]

The latter argument does have some merit when such a policy is considered as a temporary means for helping a fledgling industry—though this is not at all the case if the goal is to develop an *independent* and *competitive* industry. Moreover, the history of broadcast regulation suggests that most such "temporary" decisions tend to harden into established policy. It was just such a hardening that made this policy contribute to the perpetuation of FM radio as a service ancillary to the dominant AM system.

2. Independent Programming

The FCC dropped an initial attempt to require FM stations to program independently for a small part of the day. The Commission did not reconsider until the mid-sixties, and then under a restricted form.

When it first authorized commercial FM development in 1940, the Commission required FM stations to develop their own programming for two hours each day. This order was rescinded in 1945. In his dissenting statement to this decision Commissioner C.J. Durr (U.S. Congress, Senate, 1944) expressed a strong concern for what this ruling might do to the chances for establishing an independent FM service. According to him,

> Because of the failure of the Commission to require any independent programming of FM stations, I am very much afraid that many FM licensees who are now operating FM licenses primarily as insurance policies protecting their AM operators against the risks of technological development, with the result that . . . the listening public will receive little more than the same program traffic carried on improved highways . . . the use of two radio channels for only one program service is not only a waste of frequencies but will retard the development of FM broadcasting. (p. 5)

This policy of allowing FM stations to fully duplicate AM programming, like many other policies, became established over time and contributed to the maintenance of the FM industry in an inferior position relative to the dominant radio service. The Commission slowly changed this policy in the 1960s, but the ensuing furor from FM station owners (most of whom also owned AM stations and used FM as a duplication source) led the Commission to approve a waiver procedure for many stations, ostensibly to ease the problem of FM program development.

---

[5]That NBC regarded FM as such an ancillary service is evident from its most optimistic pronouncements on the service. It was considered "a method of radio transmission which promises, not a new type of program but improved reception of sound in many localities" (The National Broadcasting Company, *N.B.C. in 1943: Annual Review*, p. 23).

3.   AM "Drop Ins"

The FCC continued to create new AM station assignments or "drop ins," despite frequent references to overcrowding in the AM spectrum area. For example, in 1949 the Commission reported (U.S. FCC, *Annual Report: 1949*):

> Standard (AM) broadcast authorizations climbed to nearly 2200. However, fewer AM stations were authorized than in 1948. Greater difficulty was experienced in wedging into this now very saturated band. (p. 2)

Despite this perceived difficulty, the FCC continued its policy of dropping in AM stations by reducing channel separation distances and by extending the "standard" broadcast band from 550 to 540 kHz. This policy continued well into the 1950s despite the stagnation of the FM industry (U.S. Congress, Senate, 1954, pp. 1062–63). It was not until 1970 that the Commission decided to "consider" the FM service before issuing AM licenses (U.S. FCC, *Annual Report: 1970*, p. 43).

Goldin has contended in an interview in December, 1971, that, although this is certainly an indication of the Commission's preference for AM, preference should not be overlooked as an important advance in the system simply because the FM service did not benefit from it. In other words, the significant increase in the number of AM stations should itself be considered important. It is true that the number of AM stations grew from 764 in 1939 to more than 4500 in 1976 (*Broadcasting Yearbook: 1977*, p. C–312). Nevertheless, it is necessary to temper Goldin's remarks with the additional consideration that over the same period of time the number of AM chains (multiple AM station operations) has increased ninefold—from 39 in 1939 (Agee, 1949, p. 414) to more than 340 in 1976 (*Broadcasting Yearbook 1977*, pp. A-34–A-44). More than one out of every three AM stations is currently part of a chain of such stations. As former FCC Commissioner Nicholas Johnson (1970), has noted:

> The principal national sources of news are the wire services, AP and UPI, and the broadcast networks. Each of the wire services serves on the order of 1200 newspapers and 3000 radio and television stations. Most local newspapers and radio stations offer little more than wire service copy as far as national and international news is concerned. To that extent one can take little heart for "diversity" from the oft-proffered statistics on proliferating radio stations. (p. 53)

4.   "Functional" Music

As the FCC became increasingly aware of the declining fortunes of FM broadcasters, it sought to help them by encouraging the use of FM for background "functional" music through multiplex operations sanctioned by Subsidiary Communications Authorizations. Begun in 1955, these were essentially nonbroadcast permits that allowed FM licensees to program background music for stores, professional offices, and so forth, in order, in the Commission's words, "to enable commercial FM broadcasters to obtain additional revenue" (U.S. FCC, *Annual Report: 1955,* p. 6). This was later cited as a chief reason for what the Commission considered to be a "renewed interest in commercial FM" (U.S. FCC, *Annual Report: 1957,* p. 4). Although this was to some extent true of several FM stations, it did not apply to those FM stations that were independent of control by AM interests and seeking to develop independent sources of programming. Moreover, multiplexing has degraded the full tone range of FM—a possibility that the FCC alluded to in 1949 (U.S. FCC, *Annual Report: 1949,* p. 6).

THE OUTCOME

The FCC expressed optimism about the FM service just after it shifted FM to a higher spectrum area. Little delay was foreseen by the Commission (*Broadcasting,* July 2, 1945) for the development of the service:

> At the earlier hearings, some contended that FM might be delayed for two years or even longer if FM were assigned to the higher frequencies. At the time of the oral argument, June 22–23, 1945, the estimates of delays were reduced to four months. It may well be that competition will markedly reduce even this four-month estimate. (p. 68)

This optimism turned in 1948 to a concern about a leveling off of the number of FM applications and one year later to the recognition that FM was on the decline (U.S., FCC, *Annual Report: 1948,* p. 2, *1949,* p. 2). Table 5.1 indicates the leveling off of FM station licenses in the 1950s.

TABLE 5.1
Number of FM Stations, 1951–1958[a]

Year	Total FM Stations
1951	534
1952	582
1953	551
1954	529
1955	525
1956	519
1957	519
1958	526

[a]Source: U.S. FCC, *Annual Report: 1969,* p. 127.

Although the number of FM stations did grow considerably after 1958, reaching 2000 by 1970, much of this growth was due to the proliferation of Subsidiary Communications Authorizations and the increased ownership of

FM outlets by AM interests. The number of FM independent stations has grown as well, but their losses continue. (see Table 5.2)

TABLE 5.2
Economic Losses of FM Stations, 1956–1975[a]

Year	Number of independent FM stations	Number of stations reporting losses	Pre-tax *losses* of all independent FM stations (in $ millions)
1956	51	Unavailable	0.4
1957	67	"	0.5
1958	93	"	0.7
1959	148	"	1.6
1960	218	"	2.4
1961	249	"	2.6
1962	279	208	3.2
1963	294	208	3.2
1964	306	213	3.0
1965	338	236	3.3
1966	389	270	3.3
1967	405	290	4.2
1968	433	285	3.9
1969	442	306	5.5
1970	464	320	6.2
1971	527	345	9.0
1972	590	366	8.8
1973	616	377	10.0
1974	678	Unavailable	13.1
1975	703	Unavailable	9.4

[a]Sources: *Television Factbook: 1977,* p. 62-a; U.S. FCC, *Annual Report: 1974,* p. 144.

Although FM independents have generally shown losses, AM stations and FM outlets owned by AM licensees (which typically duplicate AM programming) have been profitable (see Table 5.3).

In 1945 the FCC forecast ". . . the possible establishment of several thousand FM stations within a few years after the war, or several times the number of standard broadcast stations now in operation" (U.S. FCC, *Annual Report: 1945*, p. 20). Writing shortly thereafter, Edelman (1950) foresaw the result more clearly: "FM has served principally to strengthen, rather than combat, monopoly in the broadcasting industry" (pp. 126–127). In this chapter I have tried to show how this took place.

TABLE 5.3
Earnings of AM and AM–FM Stations, 1956–1975[a]

Year	Number of AM and AM–FM stations reporting	Pre-tax *earnings* (in $ millions)
1956	2915	49.6
1957	3097	55.1
1958	3197	40.0
1959	3380	44.0
1960	3470	48.3
1961	3610	32.0
1962	3698	46.7
1963	3832	58.1
1964	3896	73.8
1965	3941	81.1
1966	4019	100.6
1967	4068	85.0
1968	4161	117.3
1969	4194	111.2
1970	4209	104.0
1971	4252	117.8
1972	4271	147.0
1973	4267	123.3
1974	4361	94.8
1975	4355	95.4

[a]Source: *Television Factbook: 1977*, No. 46.

CONCLUSION

It began with a consideration of the historical context out of which decision-making on FM radio emanated. Two elements of this context that were considered particularly significant by Commission members were the concentration of radio stations in urban areas and the increasing accumulation of industry power by the major AM networks. With these viewed as major problems by FCC members, one would have expected FM to have been treated as an important tool for the development of solutions.

However, this did not take place. First, we noted how complexity was a characteristic element of the Commission's work at this time: Not only were there many issues commanding the attention of Commissioners and staff, but several of these involved conflicting demands for scarce spectrum space. In this complex situation the Commission essentially dealt with AM and FM as separate services. It sought solutions to what were viewed as problems with the AM service solely within that area. Chief among these was the problem of monopoly. For example, a majority of Commissioners ruled that NBC had to sell one of its networks and supported the development of more clear channel stations. In addition, a Commission majority sought to avoid a repetition of the problems of AM in the FM service. Thus, strict controls were imposed on ownership of FM outlets, and limits were placed on the maximum antenna height and signal strength of FM stations. Rather than consider FM as a potential corrective to problems with the radio system, a Commission majority basically sought to avoid repeating AM problems with the FM service.

This position was particularly evident in the decision to shift FM out of its original spectrum area. The ruling was largely based on the arguments of one witness who was contradicted by several technical experts. With FM viewed as ancillary to the established system, it took merely one voice in support of the spectrum shift to justify it—a clear instance of the inference of impossibility. Next, the decision to shift FM was characterized by another common bureaucratic mechanism—the short-run/long-run split. The Commission majority essentially avoided the conflict between services by splitting them up between short- and long-run components: for the short term there would be problems with the FM service, but the shift would actually be, as it was contended, of "long-term" benefit to that service. In reality, this possibility was severely curtailed because many independent FM outlets, unable to meet the costs of conversion, were forced to sell out to major AM interests. This development was in fact stimulated by the Commission in its encouragement of FM station purchases by AM owners in order to duplicate programming.

The failure of FM to develop into a competitive challenger to AM radio was also due in part to the lack of support from dominant industry interests in this new development. This lack of support is all the more significant because the FCC lacked the resources to independently judge the value of FM radio. However, to say that the industry was united in actively opposing FM is simplistic. Though it is true that the major force in the industry, RCA, did not actively seek to make FM a primary item on the Commission's agenda, RCA did explicitly oppose both the spectrum shift and single market decisions. In fact, the Commission decided to shift FM out of its original spectrum area despite the opposition of RCA and the FCC's own panel of industry representatives, the Radio Technical Planning Board. These groups were opposed by CBS and other relatively minor industry interests.

A key point raised here is that conflicts within the industry over a specific service are frequently tied to conflicts in other areas. Thus, RCA opposed the FM spectrum shift at least in part because it did not want a precedent established that might serve as a basis for shifting the television service from the VHF area, in which RCA had major investments and a developmental edge, to the UHF area in which it would be on a par with CBS.

Although this case appears to at least partially negate a simplistic "industry capture" argument, it also points to the value of viewing that approach more systematically. For it is clear that a system that gives formal authority to an agency to make major decisions about the allocation of resources, but that also fails to support it, is essentially inviting conservative responses. Moreover, such a system provides itself with a buffer, here the FCC, made to absorb the responsbility for failing to provide the opportunity for innovations like FM to develop into competitive challengers to dominant services.

The concept of localism was an important element in the Commission majority's justification of the single market decision. Such a plan would maximize the number of local FM outlets. However, it certainly was not a concept that was consistently applied within the radio system. For example, while the Commission ostensibly sought to maximize the number of FM outlets, it was promoting the purchase of such stations by AM outlets for program duplication. It also promoted the development of AM clear channel stations that were decidedly regional in nature.

A consideration of the Commission staff is helpful in understanding the Commission's reliance on the testimony of K.A. Norton in its spectrum shift decision. Norton was the only one among radio wave propagation experts to testify before the Commission who had worked for the FCC. Although this may contribute to understanding the Commission's reliance on Norton's testimony, it is also important to recognize that Norton was currently an Army engineer and had not served with the Commission for several years.

These forces help explain how frequency modulation radio became an ancillary radio service. The next case involves a somewhat similar story in the television industry.

6

UHF: Television's Second Chance?

> . . . we are convinced that the UHF band will
> be fully utilized and that UHF stations will
> eventually compete on a favorable basis with
> stations in the VHF . . . we are convinced that
> stations in the UHF band will constitute an in-
> tegral part of a single, nationwide television
> system.
>
> U.S. FCC, 1952, p. 614

INTRODUCTION

This statement is taken from a Commission report issued over 25 years ago. It culminated twelve years of decision-making on the allocation of spectrum space to television broadcasting. Although little of the conviction has disappeared among FCC members over the years, the actual outcome has belied this optimistic forecast about the competitive potential for ultrahigh frequency television.

On the face of it, there appears to be a significant difference between FCC decision-making on FM radio and that on television broadcasting. In the former case, the Commission decided to shift FM out of its initially allocated spectrum area, ostensibly because of potential interference problems, whereas in its television decision-making, the Commission refused to shift the system out of the very-high frequency (VHF) spectrum area despite what it recognized to be an established interference problem. The difference is more apparent than real, for both are rooted in a common decision-making process. It is one that has generally characterized the FCC's response to innovations in the broadcasting market and is explored here with reference to the Commission's television station allocation policy.

Although research in this area is somewhat more extensive than that on the

FM case, one finds considerable agreement that in the television allocation case, it was the failure of the FCC to shift an assigned spectrum area that further restricted diversity in broadcasting. In particular, it has been claimed that by granting licenses for television broadcasting in the VHF area and by allowing licensed stations to retain their allocation after serious interference problems developed, the Commission limited the development of stations in the UHF area—the one area that even Commission decision-makers viewed as the only basis for a diversified national television system. For example, Moore (1973, p. 47) has argued that the television station allocation policy has been the "most damaging error" that the FCC has committed. Lewis (1964) has claimed just as strongly that

> The present system sets up dozens of UHF channels nobody wants and so few VHF channels that there has inevitably been destructive competition for them. It is, as FCC member Frederick W. Ford said recently, a "second class television system." (p. 9)

Noll, et al. (1973, p. 117) have concentrated on the FCC's standard of localism as an especially prominent force in this case. Referring to the early development of television, they contend that if the FCC had set aside its concern for localism and created a nationwide television system, based perhaps on several powerful regional centers, it would have been less costly to the economy than the present system of local station, with the added value that viewers would have about six rather than three networks from which to choose.

Although localism was considered significant in the early stages of television development, the influence of the Congress and VHF broadcasters has been viewed as more important in subsequent decisions on UHF culminating in the All-Channel Receiver Act of 1962 which specified that new television sets be equipped to receive all UHF as well as VHF channels (Giraud, Garrison, & Willis, 1971, p. 48; Webbink, 1969, pp. 543–44; U.S. Congress, House, 1962). Since that decision some have voiced renewed optimism about UHF; Krasnow and Longley (1973) claim that "no one seemed to realize how *well* the all-channel television law would work" (p. 101) and former FCC Commissioner Nicholas Johnson (1967) writes that "UHF . . . like the little engine that could appears to be climbing steadily to the top of the mountain."

How sound are these contentions? How can we explain this episode in broadcasting history?

GETTING ON THE AGENDA

Again, as in the FM case, it took what would appear to be a needlessly long time for television to reach a central position on the FCC's agenda (Cf. LeDuc, 1969; Stern, 1963a, 347–362). Of course, for many years that agenda was filled with complex issues in the radio industry. Foremost among these, as noted earlier, was the chaos that befell radio after courts had essentially negated initial attempts at federal control. It would have involved severe costs for the Commission to have shifted its attention to a new service frought with uncertainty. In addition to this, as Stern has noted, the Commission simply lacked the technical expertise to judge competing claims for the best television system (Stern, 1963b). Furthermore, there would be costs connected with a reassessment of its agenda should an early commitment to a television service by the FCC prove to be an investment in an already obsolete system. The Commission noted as early as 1939 that an early commitment to a particular form of television "may result in a high rate of obsolescence of equipment purchased by the public which may not be able to receive signals from a station that may have different standards from those now in use, or from stations employing standards which may be considerably better than those now in use or proposed to be used. . . . As a result of these two factors, considerable patience, caution, and understanding must be used at this time" (U.S. FCC, *Annual Report: 1939,* p. 45).

Soon after this statement, however, pressure on the Commission to permit the establishment of a commercial television system grew in intensity. Though the pressure was general, it was particularly strong from RCA, which under David Sarnoff had spent several years and several million dollars in an attempt to develop a television system.[1] RCA was especially influential in an organization of industry experts, the National Television System Committee, to which the FCC turned frequently in the absence of its own technical expertise.

The NTSC recommended the establishment of a system, and the Commission accepted its standards when it permitted a limited commercial television service using the VHF band in July, 1941. However, because of wartime curtailments in the domestic broadcasting industry, there were by 1944 fewer than 10,000 television receivers in use and half of these were concentrated in the New York City area.

The Commission returned to a consideration of television in 1945 and once again permitted the development of a commercial system—but not without opposition. According to an FCC report (U.S. FCC, *Annual Report: 1945)*

> Considerable controversy arose as to whether television should proceed with present channel widths in the portion of the spectrum now employed for television broadcasting (VHF) or whether emphasis should be placed on television experimentation and operation in the higher bands where wider channels are available for pictures having greater detail and color. (p. 21)

This controversy centered once again on a division within the industry. CBS,

---

[1]For a discussion of industry pressure to establish commercial television, see (U.S. Congress, Senate, 1940).

lagging behind RCA in the development of a VHF system but with investments in color TV, sought to win approval for an all-UHF system that would immediately incorporate the CBS technique for color; on the other hand, RCA, with an established VHF system, argued for either an all-VHF or a mixed system with a delay in the adoption of color standards (U.S. FCC, 1945b; cf. U.S. FCC, *Annual Report: 1946,* p. 17; *1947* pp. 78–24.

Although the conflicting parties were essentially the same as in the FM radio case, the result was different. This time the Commission sided with its panel of industry experts and RCA because a majority of Commissioners (U.S., FCC, *Annual Report: 1945*) claimed that for UHF ". . . insufficient information appeared to be available upon which to guarantee the prompt establishment of television broadcasting in this portion of the spectrum (p. 21). The Commission, however, considered the establishment of commercial television in the VHF band to be a *temporary* solution (U.S. FCC, 1945b). Why? First, it recognized that ". . . there is insufficient spectrum space below 300 mc (the VHF area) to make possible a truly nationwide and competitive television system." In addition, the Commission majority was concerned that the VHF service might be hampered by tropospheric or sky wave interference (cf. U.S. FCC, *Annual Report: 1945,* p. 85). It was therefore noted that for the "long run" television ". . . must find its lodging higher up in the spectrum (in the UHF area) where more space exists and where color and superior monochrome pictures can be developed through the use of wider channels" (U.S. FCC, 1945b). As it did in the case of radio, the Commission split the television service into short- and long-term possibilities: For the short run it authorized a VHF black and white system, whereas a UHF service was put off as a long-run possibility.

Although a similar *process* was used in the television case, the Commission took a fundamentally different *position* from that taken on FM radio. In the FM case the Commission opposed its industry panel and RCA, whereas the CBS position in favor of the spectrum shift and single market plan was supported. Here potential inteference problems were considered significant. In its support of a VHF system in the television case, the Commission reversed its earlier stance by opposing CBS and upholding its expert panel and RCA. While some concern was expressed for interference, the Commission did not consider it an overruling factor.

Despite Commission assertions that the 1945 decision represented merely a temporary commitment, VHF rapidly became the established television system. By the end of 1948 there were 51 television stations on the air and over one million sets in use (*Television Factbook,* 1973-74, No. 43, p. 77-a). Yet, the FCC's earlier expressed concern that the VHF spectrum area was inadequate for an interference-free national service proved to be well-founded as continuous "shoehorning" of VHF stations led to chaos reminiscent of the early unregulated days of radio.[2] A 1947 FCC staff memo revealed that this should not have come as a surprise to Commission members and, in addition, it linked television's problems to the FM case. In this memorandum (cited in Lessing, 1949)[3] from E.W. Allen, head of the FCC's Technical Information Division, to the Commission's Chief Engineer it is noted that:

> At present no account is taken of tropospheric transmission in the allocation of television and FM stations, although a comparable order of interference from F2 and sporadic E was the basis for the allocation of the present FM band and is now urged as a basis for shifting television upward in frequency. For the sake of consistency and sound engineering it is urged that tropospheric interference be taken into account in planning the future of television. (p. 162)

While the Commission did not discuss the obvious inconsistency between its radio and television rulings, its concern for interference led it to order a four-year halt (1948–1952) to new station licensing—the so-called "television freeze," while allocation plans were to be reevaluated. This was done, according to a Commission report "to lay the ground work for an efficient nationwide television service" (U.S. FCC, *Annual Report: 1951*, p. 114).

While one of course can never be precisely certain about interpreting such actions, it appears that the Commission, immersed in the complexity of several weighty issues and forced to rely solely on the conflicting advice of contending parties, sought to avoid the uncertainty of the untried UHF service and continued to allow sole commercial development in the established VHF area. This could be considered a safe position until the Commission was faced with what was earlier referred to as a severe "coercive fact," in this case a major disruption in the television system, which led the Commission to reconsider its commitment to the VHF area.

Significantly, however, while this reconsideration took place, the Commission allowed existing VHF television stations to continue in operation. In addition to this, the demand for television continued to rise during the years of the freeze. The 1.2 million receivers in 1948 grew to 15 million by the end of the freeze in 1952 (*Television Factbook*, 1973–1974, p. 77-a). This increase in VHF receiver ownership combined with the scarcity of stations resulting from the freeze increased the value of operating VHF stations considerably. This in turn made it all the more difficult to consider shifting all television to the UHF area. Thus, the very mechanism used by the Commission to reevaluate its agenda—the television freeze—severely constrained the kinds of possibilities that could be incorporated into a revised agenda.

The aftermath of the freeze order was that the FCC essentially reaffirmed

---

[2]For a description of the problems encountered, see Lessing (1949, p. 127) and (U.S. FCC, *Annual Report: 1949*, pp. 144–45).

[3]Lessing further notes that this memo was found by a Senate subcommittee staff member who claimed that it was tucked away in the FCC's confidential files.

the short-run/long-run policy that it had earlier accepted by approving a mixed VHF–UHF system with channels 2–13 reserved for broadcasting in the VHF band and 14–83 for UHF (U.S. FCC, 1952). While recognizing that UHF stations would operate at a great disadvantage in the short-run, particularly because few receivers capable of picking up UHF signals were being produced, the Commission exhibited a sense of optimism strikingly similar to that shown in the FM case. It claimed that ". . . there is no reason to believe that American science will not produce the equipment necessary for the fullest development of the UHF" (p. 664).

Despite similarities in the ways in which the FCC approached UHF and FM, the Commission attempted to disassociate the former from the latter, which was, in 1952, in the midst of a decline. According to the Commission's allocation *Report and Order,* "The UHF is not faced, as was FM, with a fully matured competing service. In many cases UHF will carry the complete burden of providing television service, while in other areas it will be essential for providing competitive service" (p. 624).

Further evidence of this optimism is clearly expressed in the Commission's 1952 Annual Report. Here, successful development of UHF TV was considered to be a certainty. The Commission foresaw ". . . the sudden surge of interest in UHF television. Manufacturers of transmitters announced that suitable equipment would be available and receiver manufacturers demonstrated that they had solved the problem of UHF reception" (U.S. FCC, *Annual Report: 1952,* p. 112). Thus, in 1952, the Commission concentrated on the "long-term" view that UHF would satisfy the demand for a national television service.

The Commission considered the latter concept, a national television service, to be attainable through its policy of localism, i.e., the assignment of stations in as many communities as technically feasible throughout the country. This is explicitly stated in the Commission's response to the contention of the DuMont Company that such a policy would actually limit the number of channels in each community and would therefore prohibit the growth of a multiple network system. DuMont sought a system based on the establishment of high powered regional stations which would allow DuMont and other interests to increase network competition and stimulate program diversity. Responding to this contention, the FCC (U.S. FCC, 1952) argued that:

> the Commission cannot agree with the DuMont principle that an overriding and paramount objective of a national television assignment plan should be the assignment of four commercial VHF stations to as many of the major markets as possible . . .
>
> In the Commission's view as many communities as possible should have the opportunity of enjoying the advantages that derive from having local outlets that will be responsive to local needs.   (p. 621)

Localism therefore appears to have been an important consideration in the Commission's UHF decision-making.

In addition to this, it is important to consider how the decision proved helpful to one particular established industry interest, RCA. RCA had directed the overwhelming amount of its research and development on television in the VHF area. It owned more of the valuable prefreeze VHF stations than any other company. CBS, ABC, and DuMont lagged behind in the VHF area and looked to the geographical separation of the VHF and UHF services to open up the latter as a profitable source of investment (primarily CBS) or looked to the establishment of a regional VHF system to facilitate the growth of new networks (primarily DuMont). Thus, while it cannot be said that "the industry," understood in a monolithic sense, pressured the FCC to allocate the spectrum and assign stations in the specific way that it did, it is important to recognize that a major force in that industry benefited significantly from the final result.

RCA also benefited from the final result of the FCC's surprising 1948 decision to take up the issue of color television. This issue is not only important because the outcome solidified RCA's position, but also because it is an example of how some of the complexity in TV decision-making was created by the Commission itself. At the very time when the Commission was faced with the problem of an interference-ridden television system, it is remarkable that it took up the question of standards for *color* television. According to a Congressional report (U.S. Congress, Senate, 1955b): "Although the September 1948 freeze was occasioned by the uncovering of new propagation data, the Commission decided to postpone this phase of its proceedings in order to take another look at color" (p. 3). "Another look" involved a five-year struggle, primarily between RCA and CBS, before the Commission and in the courts with systems accepted then rejected until RCA won out in 1953.

In summary, mired in this complexity, some of which was of its own creation, the FCC chose a path of low uncertainty. All major markets would have enough stations to make a two- or three-network system feasible on the established VHF system. Very few areas would have to rely solely on the untried UHF service for television.

THE AFTERMATH: DECLINE AND "PROTECTION"

It did not take long for evidence of a serious problem with the UHF service to appear. Of 81 television stations that went off the air in 1954, 69 were UHF outlets; of seven station authorizations relinquished, six of these belonged to UHF interests (U.S. FCC, *Annual Report: 1954*, p. 91). While recognizing the difficulty, the Commission (U.S. Congress, Senate, 1958a) did not connect it to its own policy. According to Commissioner Sterling:

I do not believe that the Commission can be blamed for those who display bad business judgement in trying to move in on the UHF channels without making a thorough assessment of the availability of equipment both for receiving and transmitting as well as the economic factors which they might be confronted with in the communities in which they propose to establish service. (p. 51).

Sterling did not discuss the Commission's own rosy forecasts for UHF, nor its own contribution to the creation of a system where, in most cases, the only good business judgment for prospective UHF operators would be to stay out of the market.

By 1955, the situation had worsened to the point where over 100 UHF operations had been canceled. Actually, only one-third of 325 UHF station grants had by this time been turned into operating stations. A Congressional staff report (U.S., Congress, Senate, 1955b) referred to the UHF service as an "economic blight" and expressed the fear that "UHF may well go the way of FM" (pp. 5–8). In this same year the Commission itself viewed the UHF situation as "a critical one" (U.S. FCC, *Annual Report: 1955,* p. 9).

The FCC's conception of this critical problem is perhaps even more interesting: The Commission considered it to be a "failure of UHF stations to become integrated with established VHF stations" (p. 95). The problem was not the failure of UHF outlets to become an independent force in broadcasting, but rather their inability to supplement the VHF system. Again, the FCC linked UHF's problems to economic difficulties rather than to the Commission's own contribution to the structure of the system. According to a Commission report (U.S. FCC, *Annual Report: 1956*), "To an appreciable extent these problems are basically economic and arise out of the inability, at the present stage of TV development, to obtain sufficient economic support to meet the high costs of construction, programming and operation of stations" (p. 94). It was not until 1958 that the Commission recognized "the headstart by the VHF system" as a major reason for the failure of UHF stations (U.S. FCC, *Annual Report: 1958,* p. 102).

During these years following the issuance of the 1952 station allocation plan, decisions in several areas solidified the position of UHF as an ancillary television service.

1. Deintermixture

Krasnow and Longley (1973, pp. 98ff.) claim that the FCC's concern for UHF was evidenced by Commission attempts to establish several all-UHF markets. By "deintermixing" all or several markets, UHF stations would not have to overcome the competitive advantage of VHF outlets located in the same community. Actually, deintermixture was proposed by industry interests as well as by several government officials during the 1950s.

As early as 1951, CBS proposed (*Broadcasting,* September 10, 1951, p. 78) making Chicago, Boston, and San Francisco all-UHF markets. Testifying before the Senate Commerce Committee, Frank Stanton, President of CBS,

argued that (U.S. Congress, Senate, 1954) that ". . . such a program of deintermixture may well be the only workable solution to the present UHF difficulties. Full opportunity for network competition among at least four networks would thus be assured" (p. 978). Perhaps more importantly, CBS did
not, at this time, own its legally permissible five VHF stations and was therefore interested in maintaining UHF as a valuable investment area. In addition
to CBS, both the DuMont network, (U.S. Congress, Senate, 1958a, pp. 97–
101) and the Senate Commerce Committee (U.S. Congress, Senate, 1955b;
1958a, p. 53) proposed all-UHF markets in the mid-fifties.[4] In a widely circu-
lated memorandum, the majority counsel of the Commerce Committee contended that deintermixture was essential to the survival of UHF television
(U.S. Congress, Senate, 1955b, p. 12). Furthermore, the memo criticizes the
Commission's policy on deintermixture because of several cases in which
formal proposals were presented to the FCC, ". . . all but one have been
summarily denied without a hearing on the ground that the VHF applicants
have already expended large sums of money in prosecuting their applications . . ." (p. 11). By the end of 1955 the Commission had rejected all 35
petitions for deintermixture. Overruling considerations was the harm a majority of Commissioners claimed would be done not only to established VHF stations which would be relocated, but also to VHF applicants who had invested
time and money in attempting to acquire stations (*Broadcasting*, November
14, 1955, p. 27; U.S. Congress, Senate, 1956a, pp. 333–34, U.S. FCC, *Annual Report: 1955*, pp. 95–96). Again the Commission responded
conservatively—rejecting this proposal because it would tamper with the established television system.

2. Satellites

In the early 1950s the Commission proposed to license stations strictly to
rebroadcast the programming of other television stations and thereby increase
the latters' audience and revenue (U.S. FCC, *Annual Report: 1954*, p. 92).
Such satellite stations were considered by the commission to be a potential
source of growth for UHF outlets (U.S. FCC, *Annual Report: 1955*, p. 96).
However, while some such stations did develop, most were used to rebroadcast VHF programming: The very first satellite authorization, granted in 1954,
was awarded to a company operating a *VHF* channel in Lufkin, Texas that
planned to rebroadcast the programs of a *VHF* station in Houston. Of nineteen
such stations brought into operation by mid-1957, fourteen were rebroadcasting for VHF stations and five for UHF stations (U.S. Congress, House,

---

[4]I am indebted to Mr. Nicholas Zapple, Counsel to the Senate Commerce Committee, for his
help in this area. He worked for the Committee during the period in which deintermixture was a
significant issue.

1958c, p. 34; cf. *Broadcasting,* November 11, 1956, pp. 88–89). In 1956 an organization representing UHF stations actually called on the FCC to discontinue its satellite policy because it would "prove disastrously injurious to independent UHF operations" since the latter would have to deal with the additional problem of competing with VHF satellites (U.S. Congress, Senate, 1956a, p. 331).

Once again, the Commission showed little evidence of having profited from its experience with FM radio stations that served merely as satellite adjuncts rebroadcasting the programming of AM stations. That experience should have indicated quite clearly that there was little likelihood that VHF stations would use satellite grants to develop UHF markets in those areas already served by VHF. Furthermore, it should have indicated that UHF satellites duplicating VHF programming in areas already served by VHF would do little to stimulate equipping television sets with a UHF capability. While UHF satellites might stimulate development in areas without any other television service, such grants were rare (cf. Brinton, 1962, p. 278).

3. The Station Ownership Rule

In the mid-1950s the FCC increased the number of television stations that it would permit one owner to hold to seven, provided that two of these were UHF stations (U.S. FCC, *Annual Report: 1954,* p. 91). This policy was supported by both NBC and CBS which proceeded to buy UHF stations (*Broadcasting,* January 10, 1955, p. 27; March 14, 1955, p. 72; July 11, 1955, p. 86). This did not directly assist the development of an independent UHF television system, but did help some failing stations to survive as VHF adjuncts. However, the boost provided to UHF was often short-lived. For example, all of the UHF stations purchased by NBC and CBS were dropped a few years later (U.S. Congress, House, 1958c, pp. 560, 563, 570).

4. More VHF Space, "Drop-Ins," and the Long-Run

The FCC tried to both increase the amount of VHF spectrum space available for television, as well as squeeze in more VHF stations by reducing the minimum distances separating channels. The Commission sought to increase the available spectrum space for VHF television by using space initially allocated to the Defense Department. The Office of Defense Mobilization rebuffed these attempts in both 1956 and 1960 (U.S. FCC, *Annual Report: 1956,* p. 160; *Annual Report: 1960,* p. 44).[5]

Another approach to generating more VHF stations met with greater suc-

---

[5]It is interesting that in both cases the FCC added that this would lead it to shift all television to the UHF area.

cess, but also severe criticism. In 1956 the Commission decided to decrease its minimum city-to-city mileage separation requirements for VHF stations to create new "drop-in" stations (U.S. FCC, *Annual Report: 1956,* p. 97). The Commission came under strong Congressional criticism for this policy: Many wondered how the Commission would be able to deal with the UHF problem if it continued to drop VHF stations into communities (U.S. Congress, Senate, 1958a, pp. 65–66; 1956a, pp. 406–409).

This is another example of the Commission's tendency to split services into short and long-term components. For at the same time that the Commission was announcing its "drop-in" policy, it recognized that a proposal ". . .shifting all or a major portion of VHF operations to the UHF band . . . was the only one . . . which gave promise of achieving, through the operation of the allocation processes, the long-term goal" (U.S. FCC, *Annual Report: 1956,* pp. 95–96). Again, in 1957 (U.S. FCC, *Annual Report: 1957)* it noted that a "proposal to shift all TV broadcasting . . . to UHF offered the most hope for a long-range solution" (p. 107). This long-range concern led to the creation of an industry advisory body, the Television Allocation Study Organization, charged with exploring the feasibility of such a transition. Thus, while the UHF service was considered the long-term alternative, the Commission continued "as an immediate measure" to stretch its standards and assign more VHF stations—an action which might meet immediate demand, but that would make it all the more difficult to transfer to a predominantly UHF television system. Nevertheless, despite continued recognition that the VHF spectrum area was insufficient for "a competitive TV system for the Nation's growing needs," and despite assertions that the UHF area alone could provide a long-term solution, the Commission continued its VHF "drop-in" policy into the 1960s (U.S. FCC, *Annual Report: 1960,* pp. 44–45; *Annual Report: 1962,* p. 60).

5. All-Channel Receivers

Any serious concern for all-UHF television was dropped in 1962 with passage of an act requiring that all receivers manufactured after April 30, 1964 be equipped to receive all VHF and UHF channels. Although it is true that the All-Channel Receiver Act was strongly supported by the Commission at this time, it must also be noted that there was little opposition from either the Congress or the broadcasting industry on this issue. Similar legislation was proposed by the House Judiciary Committee several times during the 1950s (U.S. Congress, House, 1957, p. 9). The television industry was nearly unanimous in its support (Krasnow & Longley, 1973, pp. 100–101). With characteristic optimism, the Commission enthusiastically viewed the production of receivers equipped with the full UHF band as the key that "would accomplish the long-range objective'' and make it unnecessary to consider a total or even partial shift of television to the UHF spectrum area[6] (U.S. FCC, *Annual Report: 1962*, p. 61, cf. pp. 4 and 24–25).

THE CONTINUING DECLINE

Despite the optimism, the inability of UHF stations to develop has continued. In 1962, the year in which the All-Channel Act was passed, there were 1537 channel assignments available for UHF stations and 683 available for VHF broadcasting. Of the 1537 reserved for UHF, only 104 were operating stations and 100 more that were once in operation had subsequently gone off the air. Of the 683 potential VHF stations, 508 were on the air and generating substantially greater revenue than operating UHF stations (U.S. FCC, *Annual Report: 1962*, p. 4). The situation did not improve even after a sharp increase in the number of sets capable of receiving UHF signals. In 1971, a year in which slightly more than 75% of television sets were equipped to receive UHF programming (U.S. FCC, *Annual Report: 1971, p. 37*), *only 301 of 1185 available UHF stations were operating. On the VHF side, 598 of 716 station reservations were in operation (Broadcasting,* September 27, 1961, p. 60).[7] As a result, in 154 of 292 broadcasting markets (representing 20% of all households), two or fewer television signals were available (*Television Factbook: 1973–1974*, pp. 62-a–70-a).

The plight of the commercial UHF broadcaster who was able to remain on the air becomes all the more clear when information on earnings is considered. The data in Table 6.1 compares the earnings of UHF stations with VHF stations owned and operated by the major networks, and with nonnetwork owned VHF stations which may or may not be affiliated with the networks.

These data indicate that while the number of operating UHF stations has increased since the early 1960s, the losses sustained by these stations have increased at an even more rapid pace—at least up until the last year for which data are available when UHF stations turned a profit for the first time since 1964. These data, however, do not register the significance of the difficulty for a particular group of commercial UHF stations that one would expect to be a major source of program diversity—those unaffiliated with any of the three major networks: In 1973 there were 53 such stations in operation and of these 16 reported a profit (U.S. FCC, *Annual Report: 1974*, p. 127).[8]

---

[6]It was claimed that the Act was "expected to do more to extend TV service than anything else in that industry's 21 years of operation."

[7]These data include noncommercial operations. For commercial stations alone, 186 of 662 UHFs were operating and 511 of 593 VHFs were on the air.

[8]Of those commercial UHF stations with a network affiliation, 61 or 112 reported a profit.

TABLE 6.1
Annual Earnings of Television Stations, 1953–1975[a]

Year	UHF Stations Stations reporting	UHF Stations Pretax earnings (in $ million)	No. Nets	Nonnetwork owned and operated VHF stations Stations reporting	Nonnetwork owned and operated VHF stations Pretax earnings (in $ million)	Non-network owned and operated VHF stations Stations reporting	Non-network owned and operated VHF stations Pretax earnings (in $ million)
1953	112	(6.3)[b]	4	16	18.0	206	56.3
1954	125	(3.8)	4	16	36.5	269	63.8
1955	103	(4.5)	4[c]	16[c]	68.0	318	86.7
1956	95	(1.9)	3	16[d]	85.4	324	106.1
1957	88	(3.5)	3	16[d]	70.7	397	92.8
1958	79	(2.2)	3	19[e]	77.0	416	97.1
1959	77	(0.5)	3	17[f]	87.9	427	134.9
1960	76	0.3	3	15	95.2	439	148.6
1961	81	(0.6)	3	15	87.0	444	150.6
1962	83	0.9	3	15	111.4	456	199.3
1963	86	0.2	3	15	136.2	464	206.8
1964	92	2.7	3	15	156.5	468	256.4
1965	100	(0.2)	3	15	161.6	473	286.5
1966	114	(7.4)	3	15	186.8	479	313.5
1967	133	(17.7)	3	15	160.1	471	272.2
1968	154	(29.5)	3	15	178.8	473	345.6
1969	169	(43.2)	3	15	226.1	489	370.7
1970	180	(45.5)	3	15	167.5	491	331.9
1971	182	(32.7)	3	15	144.9	491	277.0
1972	173	(15.9)	3	15	213.4	475	354.7
1973	177	(7.7)	3	15	287.7	489	373.1
1974	175	(6.1)	3	15	330.8	479	413.6
1975	177	9.9	3	15	314.2	477	456.2

[a]Source: *Television Factbook: 1977*, p. 53-a.
[b]Parentheses indicate losses.
[c]After September 15, 1955 the DuMont network ceased operations leaving today's three networks.
[d]Includes one UHF station.
[e]Includes three UHF stations.
[f]Includes two UHF stations.

It is apparent that even with an increase in the available sources for receiving UHF programming, the service continues to have a difficult time establishing itself as a serious competitor to the VHF system. This should not be surprising, however, considering the extent to which the Commission has protected its initial promotion of VHF television.

CONCLUSION

Consideration of the UHF television case began with a discussion of the difficulties that it had in getting on the Commission's agenda. Such elements as the Commission's lack of expertise in the face of complex issues related to both the established radio industry and the new television service, and the pressure that RCA brought to bear through the National Television System Committee were particularly important. These early developments helped make VHF television the dominant service. Television on the UHF band has remained a decidedly ancillary service.

Just as in the FM case, the Commission responded conservatively to this broadcasting innovation. Until the time of the so-called television freeze of 1948, Commissioners appeared to be avoiding the uncertainty of moving television to the UHF area despite the recognition, clearly discussed in Commission reports, that the VHF area was inadequate for the development of a national television system. Typically, it was not until the Commission was faced with a severe "coercive fact," i.e., a serious disruption in the attempt to establish a national television system on VHF, that the Commission turned to the UHF alternative. However, again typically, Commission members did not shift the entire television system to UHF but rather developed a mixed alternative. This alternative relegated UHF to a secondary position in part because the freeze itself significantly increased the value of established VHF stations.

The 1952 decision exemplified other bureaucratic mechanisms used in FM decision-making. Among these was a reaffirmation of the short-run/long-run split between services—with UHF considered the future alternative. The Commission majority essentially ignored the lessons of the FM case. It was clearly aware of the latter, but claimed that the UHF case represented an entirely different situation. In addition, the Commission mired itself in a good deal of complexity as it sought to deal with the difficult problem of color television, while most people were unable to receive any television service at all.

The Commission's commitment to localism and its tendency to bend to the pressure of powerful industry interests are significant. Television stations, both VHF and UHF, were allocated in such a way as to assure there would be stations in a large number of communities. Furthermore, the major force in the industry, RCA, benefited significantly from this approach. By intermixing VHF and UHF stations, the outlets controlled by RCA were practically assured of maintaining their dominance. Perhaps more importantly, the allocation of stations on a local basis almost guaranteed that a maximum of three national networks would be feasible. This reduction of competition, soon made evident by the demise of DuMont's efforts to build a network of UHF stations, was very beneficial to RCA.

CBS also benefited from these decisions. However, it would be overly simplistic to view the television station allocation policy as one brought about by unified industry pressure: Just as in the FM case, there was a split in the industry between RCA and CBS with DuMont adding to the conflict. CBS actually supported the move to an all-UHF system, largely because it lagged behind RCA in the development of VHF and sought to establish a UHF system using its color technique. DuMont wanted an entirely different allocation plan based on high-powered regional VHF stations that could accomodate five or six networks. Nevertheless, while there was industry conflict reminiscent of the FM case, in this situation, RCA won out as a localized VHF system became the dominant force in television.

The remainder of this chapter considered how the dominance of VHF over UHF has been maintained in part by Commission decision-making over the last two decades. Decisions on deintermixture, satellite stations, the station ownership rule, VHF "drop-ins," and the All-Channel Receiver Act exemplified this. It is interesting to note that up until passage of the all-channel law, a Commission majority considered UHF the long-term home for all of television broadcasting while continuing to support VHF—for the short run. The case of cable television is strikingly similar.

7
Cable Television: The Electronic Revolution Short-Circuited

> Broadband communications is the tool not only to provide the means for new styles in human settlements, but also to rebuild, in a sociological sense, the crowded inner core of major cities. Broadband communications systems using cable can be structured to promote small, self-determining communities within the massive metropolis. Through these, city dwellers find order, identifiable territory, community pride, and opportunity to participate and vote on matters that can be of local option—education, cultural pursuits, recreational interests, etc.
>
> ELECTRONIC INDUSTRIES ASSOCIATION (1969)

INTRODUCTION

This statement refers to a commonly described vision that generally includes such diverse elements as the videophone, electronic mail and newspaper delivery, instantaneous national opinion sampling, and many others. This chapter is concerned with how the Federal Communications Commission has dealt with one element of that vision—cable television, or what another visionary has called "the electronic communications highway" (Smith, 1972).

While there have appeared many articles containing such titles as "The Golden Antenna of CATV" (*Dunn's Review,* May 1965, p. 44) and "CATV, The Communications Revolution" (*Television Digest,* 1965, p. 2), not all the work on cable television expresses such exuberance. There have been a few more sober comparative studies including cable television (for one example, see Park, 1971), but most have been single case studies. Many of these have been efforts to assess the potential of CATV to provide a number of diverse communcations functions.[1] Some interesting work has been done on the local implementation of cable systems and community involvement in local decisionmaking in such areas as system franchising and program production (Baer, 1973; Mason et al., 1972; Price & Wicklein, 1972).

Few studies have primarily been concerned with the regulation of cable television. There have been attempts to assess the impact of the FCC's conception of a localized broadcasting system on CATV development. For example, Le Duc (1973) has contended that localism has been harmful to the growth of CATV: "Since these community systems, like clear channel and network services before them, would perform a function of program delivery not related to that objective (i.e., localism) they could be viewed at best as an extraneous element in the broadcast structure" (p. 59).[2] While the evidence does not support his inclusion of network services in this statement, the issue of localism versus CATV is an important one to be addressed subsequently.

Others have concentrated on the role of the major commercial broadcasters in cable decision-making. These analysts have generally claimed that broadcasters have influenced the FCC to restrict the development of cable, particularly in population-dense markets. Much of this work echoes the claim of Smith (1972) that in CATV policy-making ". . . the Commission has defined the public interest as the perpetuation of the over-the-air television industry as it now exists" (p. 45).[3]

Few studies have considered the internal operations of the Commission of major consequence in its CATV decision-making. Among those that have is an interesting analysis of the influence that the Cable Television Bureau staff at the FCC has exerted on Commission rulings in order to promote cable development (Berner, 1974, pp. 141–81).

Turning to the Commission's action on CATV, while the first inspection of a cable system by an FCC engineer took place in 1949, it was not until the late 1950s that the Commission began to seriously consider CATV. In 1959, the FCC declined to assume regulatory authority over cable television in a case involving cable system access to microwave facilities (U.S. FCC, 1959a). However, this decision was partially reversed in 1962 when the Commission decided to assert jurisdiction over CATV microwave suppliers (U.S. FCC, 1962). The determination to take on regulatory responsibility for cable systems was formalized in the FCC's First Report and Order (U.S. FCC, 1965a). Specific rules, particularly regarding the carriage of broadcast signals by CATV systems, were outlined in the 1966 Second Report and Order (U.S.

[1] Among these have been studies from Rand such as Feldman (1971), and Goldhamer (1970). Also included among analyses that have focused on future potential are Sloan Commission on Cable Communications (1971) and Smith (1972).

[2] Cf. Johnson (1970) and Noll et al. (1973, pp. 162–63).

[3] Cf. Le Duc (1969), Moore (1973, pp. 64–70), and Berner (1974, pp. 78–80).

FCC, 1966). Finally, in 1972, the Commission issued the major statement of its policy on CATV (U.S. FCC, 1972a).

Consideration of this case begins, as did the other two, with a discussion of the difficulty that cable television had in getting on the FCC's agenda of items worth its serious attention. Following this, we turn to how cable was treated once it became such an agenda item. The difference between viewing cable as a component along with broadcasting in a total communications system, and viewing cable as, at best, ancillary to the established broadcasting system is particularly important here. Finally, the impact of the latter view on the development of cable television is considered.

GETTING ON THE AGENDA

Small Town Service

It is significant that cable began merely as a service that could enhance the quality of television signals for communities located on the fringes of good broadcast reception. Typical among these was the Panther Valley Television Company founded by Robert Tarlton of Lansford, Pennsylvania in the early 1950s. Lansford is a small community located about 65 miles from Philadelphia—too great a distance for adequate broadcast television reception. Tarlton and his associates dealt with this problem by building a tall master antenna on a mountain to pick up the faint signals from Philadelphia stations. These were amplified and fed into coaxial cables ultimately connected to the homes of people subscribing to the service. For a $125 installation fee and $3 monthly service charge, Lansford area residents received the three Philadelphia stations with clearer pictures than did most suburban Philadelphia residents. CATV thereby became identified as a service that would simply boost the quality of broadcast signals for small communities. This identification made the service easier to ignore at the FCC: Certainly this was not a serious threat and especially not a potential major contributor to the burgeoning television system.

Interference and Economic Nuisance

Nevertheless, as Lansford-like systems began to proliferate, the Commission began to express concern about whether such systems might pose interference or economic problems to neighboring broadcasting stations (U.S. FCC, *Annual Report: 1953,* p. 98; *1954,* pp. 92–95; *1955,* p. 99; *1956, pp.* 99–100; U.S. FCC, 1956). CATV itself was not singled out as a potential problem, but was viewed along with several other ancillary services whose appearance at this time might have been considered problematic. A 1958 FCC analysis addresses this concern: CATV, just as satellite stations, translators, and boosters, was an auxiliary system whose potential negative impact on the established broadcasting service was to be considered by the Commission. More specifically, it noted that (U.S. FCC, *Annual Report: 1958*):

> While the rise of these various kinds of facilities provides a means of extending TV service to small communities lacking local stations and to areas beyond the range of satisfactory TV service, all of them pose problems, in greater or lesser degree relating to their competitive impact on regular TV stations. (p. 108)

As early as 1958 the Commission began expressing concern that this auxiliary service might hurt "regular" TV. Given the initial small-town role of cable systems and the complexity of the FCC's work in trying to establish a nationwide television service through the 1950s, it was easier for the Commission to link CATV to potentially harmful auxiliary services rather than consider it as a possible solution to its television problems.

Temporary Aberration

An additional factor reinforcing CATV's ancillary position was that it could and *was* easily looked upon as a temporary aberration providing service until such time as a national broadcasting television service could be established (U.S. FCC, 1959b). Since, as discussed in the last chapter, the Commission felt that it would only be a few years before the VHF–UHF system was fully developed, it was not necessary for the Commission to spend any more time on cable than necessary to make certain that CATV systems would not threaten the full development of the broadcasting system. The Commission was not alone in its consideration of CATV as a temporary development. According to a 1959 report of the Senate Commerce Committee (U.S. Congress, Senate, 1959a),

> When the TV freeze was lifted in 1952, it was widely felt that the community antenna system, having provided a valuable interim service, would disappear when faced with the competition of many new stations which were expected shortly to blanket the country with local service. (p. 3)

No Time to Waste on CATV

The idea that the FCC considered it unnecessary to spend its time on CATV is important: Under the assumptions of analytic approaches to the study of organizations, time is all too frequently viewed as infinitely available, rather than as a potential significant constraint—as it may very well have been in the Commission's handling of CATV. With cable still a minor service in small communities, and with the Commission deeply involved in dealing with the declining fortunes of both FM radio and UHF television, it can be understood why the Commission would consider cable not worth the time that could be better spent on more pressing issues. The Commission in fact discussed this on several occasions in the late 1950s. For example, in 1958 the Commission claimed (U.S. Congress, Senate, 1958c) that it could not assert common carrier control over cable systems, because ". . . assertion of jurisdiction would require the regulation of rates and services of several hundred CATV systems. It would entail an administrative burden which the Commission is not equipped to handle (p. 4142). Understandably now, this is why in 1959 and thereafter the Commission opposed Congressional attempts to require the licensing of cable systems and simply sought to make cable operators get retransmission consent from stations broadcasting the programs picked up by their operations: The Commission sought to avoid the administrative burden of directly regulating another industry.

Neither Broadcasting nor Common Carrier

A further contributor to viewing CATV as at best an auxiliary service is that cable did not fit into either of the Commission's major communications categories: it was neither a common carrier nor a form of broadcasting. This was discussed by Commissioner Doerfer as early as 1955 (Doerfer, 1955) and was used as a reason by the Commission as a whole for its refusal to assert direct regulatory control over cable television in 1958 and 1959 (U.S. FCC, *Annual Report: 1958,* p. 108). Specifically, the FCC claimed that CATV could not be categorized as a common carrier service, like the telephone system, because the subscriber did not determine the nature of the signal being carried. On the other hand, it could not be considered a form of broadcasting because signal transmission was completely by wire (U.S. FCC, *1959a,* p. 426). This particular argument was used again by the Commission to justify its refusal to license individual cable systems (U.S. FCC, *Annual Report: 1965,* p. 80). Thus, rather than reorient its fundamental communications schema, the Commission simply placed cable outside of it as ancillary to the established system. Rather than consider the questions that cable raised about the usefulness of the Communications Act itself in an era of rapid technological change, the Commission simply viewed it as a minor anomaly. The result of this position, as Le Duc (1973) has noted, is that "the FCC lost both the time and the knowledge it needed to govern its growth" (p. 76). As a result, the FCC was largely unprepared to deal with the CATV industry as it turned from a community antenna to program distribution—from the marginal position of an auxiliary service to that of a potential challenger to the established system.

Harmful to Localism

Perhaps of even greater significance in the consideration of cable television as a minor service is that CATV systems did not fit the Commission's conception of a proper national television broadcasting system—one characterized by a multiplicity of local stations that could be responsive to the needs of local communities. Cable could, in fact, be looked upon as a threat to that conception, particularly when cable operators began importing distant signals into local markets and thereby lowering the audience sizes of broadcasting outlets. A 1959 FCC report expresses the concern that, as a result of this audience segmentation, CATV would drive local stations out of business and thereby eliminate service for rural residents who were dependent on local broadcast stations for service and whose geographic isolation made cable service economically unfeasible (U.S. FCC, 1959a, p. 403).

It was not just the Commission who was concerned about the impact of cable on localism. As might be expected, local broadcasters affected by the spread of cable were very upset and took their concerns to Congress. In part, as a result of this, the Senate Commerce Committee had its staff prepare a report on the effects of cable on local broadcasters. This report, written under the direction of Kenneth Cox, who later served as a member of the Commission, suggested that priorities be established among services in the following way: (1) local broadcast stations, (2) semisatellite stations, (3) pure satellite stations, (4) booster translators, (5) cable systems. The reason for this system of priorities, according to the report, was that "the Commission should always keep the goal of the greatest possible degree of local service in the forefront of all its deliberations and actions" (U.S. Congress, Senate, 1958c, pp. 48–49).

The FCC's concern for the impact of cable systems on local broadcast outlets was reiterated in 1962 (U.S. FCC, *Annual Report: 1962*):

> The Commission has become increasingly concerned over the impact of CATV operations for the survival or growth of local TV outlets and services. This concern prompted it . . . to inquire into the impact of CATVs and other adjuncts upon the development of TV broadcasting. (pp. 65–66)

Thus, cable could be considered as ancillary or "adjunct" because it could not be fit into the established conception of the "correct" television system.

The Commission was thus faced with a dilemma in the late 1950s and early 1960s: It had neither the resources nor the certainty of its jurisdiction to add a new industry to its regulatory responsibility; yet, it did not want to see its broadcast television plan hurt by the new service. While there was general Congressional agreement that the problem was a serious one, no agreement could be reached in Congress on the precise form of legislation for regulating cable systems.[4] A possible factor contributing to Congressional inaction was the lack of concern expressed by organizations such as the National Association of Broadcasters for the small broadcasting stations being affected by cable development. As was noted earlier, the Commission itself contributed to this situation by opposing Congressional attempts to have the FCC license cable systems because of the administrative burden that such regulation would entail.

The result, as is common in complex situations, was that a stopgap measure was employed—one that could provide a temporary solution to what the Commission perceived to be a growing problem. In 1962 the Commission refused to allow a microwave company to transmit broadcast signals for a cable system, the company's only customer (U.S. FCC, 1962). The Commission's reason for the ruling was that such signals would adversely affect local broadcasting outlets. Nevertheless, the Commission was quick to point out that this was not an assertion of control over all cable systems, but merely over microwave companies serving such systems.

While it is difficult, of course, to explain with certainty why this decision was taken, several important points need to be considered. First, there was not a great deal of pressure from the broadcasting industry or from the Congress for the Commission to assume control—cable systems were actually having practically no impact in major broadcasting markets. Second, there was also no unified pressure from the Commission's staff for an assertion of jurisdiction in this area. In fact, the Commission's action in the microwave case was a reversal of the decision reached by its own hearing examiner who, in May, 1961, determined that ". . . whatever impact the operations of the CATV may have . . . are matters of no significance to the ultimate determination made that a grant to . . . Carter, a bona fide communications common carrier, will serve the public interest" (Pike & Fisher, *Radio Regulation, 22,* pp. 216–217). A third, significant point is that the development of CATV, concurrent with the decline of UHF, neither led the Commission to reconsider its established television system policy nor even to study the present or future potential of the cable service. No attempt was made to consider how cable might contribute to the television service: It was treated solely as an adjunct which might prove to be detrimental to the existing system.

That this was true in the absence of powerful external or internal pressure on the Commission might appear to be surprising. This becomes more understandable by recalling our earlier discussion of how, in the face of complex issues, organizational decision-makers avoid conducting a comprehensive

[4]Particularly valuable assistance in understanding Congressional attempts to legislate cable regulation was provided by Mr. Nicholas Zapple, staff counsel to the Senate Commerce Committee in a March 1975 interview.

search for new information or new policy directions. The latter might occur if the established system were in a state of chaos; that is, were the Commission faced with a severe "coercive fact," we might expect some reevaluation of different courses of action. But in this case, with the system far from chaos, the Commission simply viewed the newcomer as a threat to its established policy and rather than initiate costly search procedures, employed a measure which both minimized its own involvement and ensured control of the CATV threat. Viewed from the perspective of an organization attempting to deal with complexity in a way that avoids the risks of major failure, it would have been surprising for the Commission to have done otherwise, particularly since this is how the Commission reacted to other broadcast market innovations.

THE CONTROL OF CABLE

FCC regulation of microwave companies is still not direct control of cable systems. The latter began as the cable "threat" grew and as potential sources of control from outside the Commission were not assertive. Specifically, the FCC did not become significantly involved in cable decision-making until CATV began to develop as a potential competitor to major broadcast television stations; until the Commission had exhausted attempts to get Congress to pass a strict retransmission consent law, and not until the courts rejected the contention that cable operators were unfair competitors because they did not make copyright payment for programming. In other words, the Commission avoided action until most other outlets were exhausted.

Le Duc (1973) has pointed to the irony of CATV's emergence as a "threat": "In essence, then, if cable appeared to be coming of age in 1964, it was also emerging from the obscurity which had protected it in the past from the full force of the broadcast industry's challenge" (p. 119). This "coming of age" amounted to a shift in the direction of the cable industry as many operators began to consider more than merely upgrading the signals broadcast into rural communities. Increasingly, cable companies were importing signals from markets beyond the nearest urban area and thereby holding out the promise of both better service *and* several more channels of programming.

As a result of this, the Commission became strongly concerned ". . . about the problems posed for free TV—especially the development of the UHF broadcast service—by the mushrooming growth of CATV systems" (U.S. FCC, *Annual Report: 1965,* p. 81). It also argued that the ". . . CATV service should be supplementary to and not cripple the local TV broadcast service or impede the growth of TV broadcasting" (p. 80). As with other innovations, the FCC did not consider revamping its conception of a "proper" system in the light of changing developments in the potential of CATV; rather, it judged cable by the negative economic impact that it might have on the established broadcasting system—now expressed increasingly in terms of the need to protect the declining UHF service.

Of course, at this time, pressure on the Commission from the broadcasting industry for direct control of cable systems grew—albeit not as a unified force. There was actually a multiplicity of industry interests. The cable industry was split between small booster operators content to remain in rural areas obscure from direct Commission control and larger interests that looked to distant signal importation and major market penetration as sources of growth. Le Duc (1973, pp. 128–29) has noted that many of these major cable interests actually sought FCC regulation in order to avoid the control of state and local governments. Of further importance is that among the larger interests there was an increasing number of broadcasters who recognized the potential of CATV and began buying into systems. This continued a pattern discussed in the last two chapters: Established broadcasters come to exercise direct control over innovations by investing needed capital in companies promoting the innovations. Finally, among broadcasters not investing in cable were small market operators directly affected by cable companies and major broadcast station owners, including the networks, who were not yet affected by market fragmentation as much as by the use of programming by cable companies without payment of copyright fees.

At the center of these conflicting pressures was the Commission, which did not act until it became clear that neither the Congress nor the courts would control the development of cable. Despite repeated pleas from the Commission (e.g., U.S. FCC, *Annual Report: 1962,* p. 26; *1964,* p. 70), the Congress was again unable to pass legislation restricting cable systems. With the Commission considered the organization responsible for positive action in this area, and with a conflict between the Chairmen of the Commerce Committees in each House, Senator Pastore and Representative Harris, it became evident that no cable control would come out of the Congress (Interview with Nicholas Zapple, 1975; Le Duc, 1973, p. 142). As for the judiciary, in 1964 a circuit court ruled that cable systems were *not* competing unfairly with broadcasters even though CATV proprietors did not pay copyright fees for broadcast programming that they picked up and used over CATV.[5]

With 1200 cable systems, serving over one million subscribers in 1964, threatening the Commission's conception of a proper national television system and with no cable control forthcoming from Congress or the courts, the Commission was left to take action on its own. The final impetus to Commission action may have come from a change in personnel that brought Newton Minow, William Henry, and Kenneth Cox, all considered "administrative activists," to the Commission. Lee Loevinger, also a Commissioner at this

[5]*Cable Vision, Inc. v. K.U.T.V., Inc.,* 335 F. 2d 348 (9th Circ., 1964).

time, though one with a decidedly different perspective on regulation, has gone as far as to contend that "In 1962, the Commission experienced a change of view (toward CATV) which was induced not by any new investigation or . . . review of facts, but simply by a change in personnel" (U.S. Congress, House, 1965, p. 41). It is true that there is no evidence to suggest a general investigation or even a search for new information—in the absence of a system breakdown such action is rare. However, this does not mean that it was solely a shift in personnel that led to Commission action. As was previously discussed, a shift in the cable industry toward distant signal importation and major market penetration along with the failure of the Congress and courts to provide the types of control that the Commission sought were major influences on FCC action. It is also important to recognize that the Commission did not actually assume jurisdiction over cable systems until it issued its *First Report and Order* in 1965, three years after Loevinger saw a shift in the FCC toward a more activist stance.

It is interesting to observe that in this ruling the Commission claimed the need to regulate CATV despite acknowledging that analysis "did not furnish the tools" to measure the damage that cable television was supposedly inflicting or could inflict on the broadcasting system. According to the Commission, ". . . unless we were convinced that the impact of CATV competition upon the broadcasting service would be negligible, we would favor some restrictions as a potential equalization of the conditions under which CATV and the broadcast service compete (U.S. FCC, 1965, p. 700). In a strange sort of logic reminiscent of that used in the FM spectrum shift situation, the Commission decided that it would take convincing evidence that cable would *not* be able to compete with broadcasting, to prevent the Commission from controlling cable.

In its decision, the Commission made licensing of cable relay stations conditioned upon the agreement of cable operators to carry the programming of each broadcast station within 60 miles of the cable system upon the request of that broadcast station. The Commission also prohibited the duplication of programming by the cable system for a period of 15 days before or after its showing by a local station. Thus, in a shift from its 1959 position, the Commission asserted its authority over cable systems despite recognizing that it lacked the analytic tools to justify its action. Summarizing the Commission's position Chairman Henry explained: "that policy is to promote CATV as a supplementary service but not to place primary reliance on it" (U.S. Congress, House, 1965, p. 32).

This position was not one taken with complete unanimity at the FCC. The dissenting view of Commissioner Loevinger is particularly interesting because it offers the analytic alternative to the FCC majority view. According to Loevinger:

What I regard as a basic error in the FCC approach is that it is negative and restrictive rather than positive and expansive. It assumes that limitations and restraints upon one mode of transmitting will necessarily benefit other modes. I think the objective should be to encourage the expansion of service . . . and this is what the Congress has told us to do.   (p. 32)

Arguing from an analytic perspective, Loevinger saw CATV and broadcasting as components of a total communications system, while the Commission majority essentially accepted the established broadcasting service as the primary system that needed protection from CATV.

This protection was extended in 1966 with the FCC's second major CATV ruling: This basically prevented CATV operators from importing distant broadcast signals in the top 100 markets (containing 90% of television households) without a Commission hearing—whether or not such operators were served by microwave common carriers. The Commission claimed that this action would protect local broadcast stations in general and particularly UHF outlets (U.S. FCC, 1966, pp. 770–78). This conclusion is challenged by reports suggesting that CATV would actually aid the development of UHF stations, particularly those outlets already in operation. According to an analysis by Martin Seiden (1972) who had prepared an economic report on CATV for the Commission in 1965,

It seems that in its desire to preclude loss of audience to *potential* UHF entrants, the Commission policy of restricting CATV entry into the major markets denied opportunities to *existing* UHF stations, unaffiliated stations, and educational stations. In view of their generally small broadcast audience potential, these kinds of stations could have benefited from wider distribution of their signals through CATV. (p. 101)[6]

This contention was supported in reports produced by Frazier, Gross, and Co. (cited in Smith, 1972, p. 51), a Washington, D.C. management consulting firm, and by Rolla Park of Rand (Park, 1971). Park also pointed to the potential benefit to UHF stations of having their transmission quality and position on the channel selection dial made comparable to that of VHF stations.

Furthermore, in attempting to protect the local broadcast service the Commission actually encouraged the control of cable companies by large corporations, including many major broadcasting interests, because the rule put many CATV companies in such a difficult economic situation that only large operators could absorb the losses that would be incurred during the period of the Commission's restrictive CATV policy. By 1968, fully 30% of all cable systems were owned by broadcasters (Le Duc, 1973, pp. 158–159).

An important point concerning this decision that has not been considered by the critics, however, is that it enabled the Commission to control cable without directly involving itself in the day-to-day regulation of CATV systems.

---

[6]His earlier work (Seiden, 1965) was prepared for the Federal Communications Commission.

The burden of proof was placed on cable systems in the top 100 markets to petition for a hearing and to show that the importation of distant signals into a local market would not adversely affect local stations in that market (U.S., FCC, *Annual Report:* 1966, p. 87). At this time there were 406 CATV systems operating in the largest 100 markets, 119 systems under construction, 500 that had been awarded franchises, and 1200 pending applications— making for a potential for over 2000 petitions for a hearing under the Commission's 1966 rules. Since the Commission did not have the staff to handle even a fraction of this potential, and since it made no effort to increase its staff in this area, the result was a general freeze on the penetration of cable systems into major market areas. In fact, only one hearing was completed, and that went against a cable system petitioning for a franchise in the San Diego area despite a plea by a San Diego *UHF* operator that cable would help UHF stations (cf. *Broadcasting,* September 1965, p. 63).[7] So much for the Commission's concern for the decline of UHF TV.

The regulation of cable without direct daily FCC involvement became more explicit in 1968 when the Commission ruled that a CATV system operating within 35 miles from the center of a top-100 market could not import signals unless it received the consent of the originating broadcasting station (U.S. FCC, 1968b). Why this restrictive ruling? The Commission saw the need to protect television broadcasting stations from the alleged unfair competitive advantage of cable systems, as well as enable the Commission to lessen its "administrative burden" because the new rules would "close down the burdensome major market hearings."

It is important to note that also in 1968 the Supreme Court upheld the Commission's right to regulate cable systems,[8] but in addition ruled that such systems were not required to make copyright payments for programming.[9] The latter ruling came as something of a surprise to the Commission[10], and its 1968 rules represent a response, if not an overruling, of the Court's decision. As *Broadcasting* magazine, never a friend to the cable industry, reported shortly after the FCC reached a decision (*Broadcasting,* December 23, 1968):

---

[7]It has been noted that several waivers of the hearing requirement were obtained "for cable systems operating in markets too small to be of particular concern to the Commission" (Berner, 1974, p. 85).

[8]*United States v. Southwestern Cable,* 392 U.S. 117 (1968).

[9]*Fortnightly Corp. v. United Artists,* 392 U.S. 390 (1968). This was determined to be true as well for cable operators who imported distant signals in *TelePrompTer Corp. v. Columbia Broadcasting System,* No. 71–1628 (March 4, 1974).

[10]This point was made clear in my interview with Henry Geller in December 1974. Mr. Geller was the Commission's General Counsel in 1968. In addition, the Commission decided in 1967 not to allow an experiment to test the impact of cable on UHF because it expected "new important developments (e.g., in the copyright field)." *Suburban Cable Television* 9 FCC 2d, 1015, Cf., "FCC Doesn't Want CATV Research," *Broadcasting* (January 15, 1968), p. 56.

> This proposal is a kind of jerry-built substitute for the decision the Supreme Court did not
> hand down last summer when it held that CATV systems do not incur copyright liabil-
> ity when they pick up and retransmit programming. It is a substitute also for legislation
> making CATV subject to copyright laws that Congress considered but did not enact this
> year. (p. 62)

Unable to get action from either the Congress or the Court to support its
broadcasting system, the FCC simply ruled on its own.

The Commission's 1968 ruling (U.S. FCC, 1968b) is of further interest because it contains an important parallel to the FM and UHF cases—a split in
services between short- and long-run possibilities. The Commission refers to
the 1968 rules as "interim" measures, while for the long run,

> broadcasting (which uses the air waves) might eventually be converted in whole or in part,
> to cable transmission . . . thereby freeing some broadcast spectrum for other uses and
> making it technically feasible to have a greater number of national and regional TV net-
> works and local outlets. (para. 9)

In addition, the Commission discussed such future developments as facsimile
reproduction of newspapers, electronic mail delivery, and cable-computer lin-
kages (para. 8). While it may be true, as Berner (1974, p. 88) has claimed,
that the Commission labeled the rules "interim" in order to avoid the Administrative Procedure Act's stipulation that all parties affected by a *final* ruling be given the opportunity to file comments prior to enactment, it is also
important to view this as another case of avoiding conflict by splitting up services into short- and long-run possibilities. Just as FM would one day be the
primary radio source, and just as one day we would be watching an all-UHF
television system, now the Commission forecast the day of a cable-dominated
television service—along with electronic mail and newspapers. However, just
as in the other cases, for the short run, the innovation—in this case
CATV—must be controlled.[11]

The period from 1968 to 1972 was marked by a curtailment in cable development, particularly in major markets, reminiscent of the 1948–52 television freeze. Both periods were also marked by the increasing involvement of
communications companies that could better absorb the short-run losses of a
freeze period. In fact, the increased interest in CATV systems by broadcasting
companies has been cited as a major reason for the decline in opposition to
cable development. As Seiden (1972, p. 7) has pointed out, the major broadcaster trade associations, such as the National Association of Broadcasters and
the Association of Maximum Service Telecasters, once in the forefront of
calls for the restriction of CATV, lessened their opposition to cable as the
proportion of NAB–AMST members, who were cable owners, passed one-

---

[11]Commissioner Robert E. Lee made this explicit shortly after the 1968 "Interim Report" was
released. See "FCC's Lee Says CATV to Stay as Is until UHF Builds," *Variety*, 5 (February,
1969).

third (Cf. Sloan, 1971 pp. 299–32). Although in 1970 the Commission did restrict broadcaster involvement in cable systems—by prohibiting network ownership of CATV and broadcaster ownership of CATV systems in their own broadcasting markets (U.S. FCC, *Annual Report:* 1970, p. 67), by June 1973, 34.6% or 1048 of 3032 cable systems in operation were owned by broadcasters and 10.2% or 308 were owned by newspaper interests (*Television Factbook: 1973–74,* p. 84-a).

During this period the Commission considered several proposals for the cable industry, including one to have CATV systems subsidize the operation of public television stations.[12] Many of these emanated from the newly created Cable Television Bureau. It was not until August 1971, however, that the Commission proposed specific new cable rules in a letter to Congress. This proposal is interesting because, while noting again that CATV systems should supplement not replace the established broadcast television service, the Commission did admit that the cable threat to UHF stations was not nearly as great as had been earlier predicted. According to the Commission (see Pike & Fisher, *Radio Regulation,* 24, 2d, 1766),

> Our own study of the matter has persuaded us that it would be wrong to halt cable development on the basis of conjectures as to its impact on UHF stations. We believe the improvements that cable will make in clearer UHF coverage will at least offset the inroads on UHF audiences made by the limited number of distant signals that our rules would permit to be carried.

What is probably of greater significance is that the final result of the Commission's decision-making process differs in a most important way from the 1971 letter. Specifically, in the 1972 *Cable Television Report and Order,* the Commission prevented cable systems in the top 50 markets from importing programming under exclusive contract to a local broadcast station for the contract's duration. A two-year limit was imposed on exclusivity in the second 50 markets and no exclusivity was recognized beyond the top 100 (U.S. FCC, 1972a). It has been estimated that the top-50 market exclusivity provision alone would black out over half of all distant programming for cable (Park, 1972, p. 6).[13] That the Commission was primarily concerned with protecting major market stations contradicts the Commission's traditionally expressed concern for small market stations.

Some have claimed that the FCC decided to continue its restrictive CATV policy because of pressure from the broadcasting industry and the White House—specifically through its controversial Office of Telecommunications Policy Director Clay T. Whitehead. Commissioner Nicholas Johnson's strong opposition to the 1972 *Report and Order,* summarizes this view clearly (in Rivkin, 1973):

---

[12]This was labeled the "public dividend" plan. (Cf. U.S. FCC, 1970b.)

[13]Cf. Chazen and Ross (1970, p. 1829) and Le Duc (1973, pp. 198–99).

In future years, when students of law and government wish to study the decision-making process at its worst, when they look for examples of industry domination of government, when they look for Presidential interference in the operation of an agency responsible to Congress, they will look to the FCC handling of the never-ending saga of cable television as a classic case study. (p. 210)[14]

On the other hand, a former member of the OTP staff has contended that the rules actually emanated from the Commission's staff who, he argues, were so accustomed to thinking in terms of the traditional broadcasting system that they were unable to clearly view "the unique opportunities and dangers of the new medium" (Owen, 1973, p. 11).

While there is support for both of these contentions, it is also important to consider the Commission majority's own lengthy explanation of the final result; for it is here that the force of uncertainty is brought to the fore. Given the complexity of the cross-cutting interests involved in cable decision-making, the Commission majority perceived that (U.S. FCC, 1972a):

there is no consensus, and we do not pretend that we can forecast too precisely how cable will evolve in major markets. There is inherent uncertainty. But this does not mean that we should stand still and block all possibility of new and diverse communications benefits. Rather, it means that we should act in a conservative, pragmatic fashion—in the sense of maintaining the present system and adding to it in a significant way, taking a sound realistic first step and then evaluating our experience. (para. 70)

The Commission acted, as it has done with other innovations in the broadcasting market, to minimize the uncertainty inherent in a complex situation. What is even more interesting is that the existence of complexity and the uncertainty brought about by no clear-cut knowledge of the results of any action probably contributed to the final agreement among the parties involved. As Owen (1973) has noted, ". . . the complexity itself may have been responsible for the success of the negotiations. At the time the compromise was reached, none of the parties, and certainly not the Government, had the slightest idea of the detailed consequences" (p. 9). Thus, to criticize the final result, as has Rolla Park of Rand, because it was developed without the use of "classical analysis" (Park, 1973, p. 71) is to fail to recognize that such analysis is often of little consequence in political decision-making; in addition, it so clearly defines the differences among parties that it heightens the problem of breaking stalemates and reaching a final result. It is often the complexity and uncertainty of decision-making situations that enable *some* action to be taken. That action in the case of CATV, as it was with FM and UHF, clearly relegated the innovation to a secondary position in the broadcasting market.

---

[14]For a good summary of how these pressures culminated in the so-called "consensus" agreement see *Broadcasting,* August 30, 1971, p. 83; October 11, 1971, p. 38; October 18, 1971, p. 7; *Television Digest,* August 23, 1971.

ECONOMIC DOLDRUMS

Regulatory policy has not been the sole force behind the inability of CATV systems to grow. Economic problems that would have hampered growth in a favorable regulatory climate continue to beset the industry. Anne Branscomb (1974, p. 10), former Communications Counsel for TelePrompter the largest cable company, has pointed to significant increases in debt service and construction costs, which inflationary pressures have made most difficult for this capital intensive industry to bear. This has become an even more acute problem as cable owners try to establish systems in high cost urban areas. Branscomb emphasizes, however, that the 1972 rules have certainly compounded the economic difficulties. According to her, ". . . non-duplication and syndicated exclusivity rules are so stringent that a careful calculation of the permitted signals in the top 100 markets discloses that there are only 17 markets in which the importation will create attractive marketing potential" (pp. 7–8).

The data in Table 7.1 on subscriber penetration by cable systems point to the difficulty that the cable industry has experienced. Two additional points of information are important to consider in the light of these data.

First, despite the fact that broadcast television had penetrated into 95% of American households by 1969 (*Television Factbook:* 1973–1974, p. 84-a), in each subsequent year, with one exception, television broadcasting has increased its market penetration by a greater number of households than have cable systems. In 1973, for example, while cable penetration increased by 1.3 million homes, broadcast television grew by 2.1 million households.[15]

Second, as the data in Table 7.2 clearly show, cable systems are still predominantly concentrated in small communities. Also, they are, to a great extent, still controlled by broadcasting, newspaper, and publishing interests (see Table 7.3).

[15]The following are absolute growth figures for 1970–75:

Year	CATV (in thousands)	Broadcast television (in thousands)
1970	900	1450
1971	800	1900
1972	700	1900
1973	1300	2100
1974	1400	1200
1975	1100	1700

Source: *Television Factbook: 1977*, pp. 66-a, 75-a.

TABLE 7.1

**Number of Subscribers to Cable Television
Systems, 1952–1976**[a]

Year	Total subscribers (in thousands)
1952	14
1953	30
1954	65
1955	150
1956	300
1957	350
1958	450
1959	550
1960	650
1961	725
1962	850
1963	950
1964	1085
1965	1275
1966	1575
1967	2100
1968	2800
1969	3600
1970	4500
1971	5300
1972	6000
1973	7300
1974	8700
1975	9800
1976	10800

[a]Source: *Television Factbook: 1977*, p. 75-a.

TABLE 7.2

U.S. CATV Systems by Subscriber Size, September 1, 1976[a]

Subscribers	Systems
50,000 and over	10
20,000–49,999	58
10,000–19,999	181
5,000– 9,999	345
3,500– 4,999	243
1,000– 3,499	1164
250– 999	1216
249 and under	472
not available	26
	3715

[a]Source: *Television Factbook: 1977*, p. 75-a.

TABLE 7.3

Ownership of CATV Systems[a]

Category	Systems	%
Broadcaster	1183	31.8
Newspaper	476	13.0
Publisher	492	13.2
Program producer or distributer	729	19.6
Theater	313	8.4
Telephone	69	1.8
Community or subscriber	96	2.6
Manufacturer	455	12.2

[a]Source: *Television Factbook: 1977*, p. 73-a. Figures as of September 1, 1976.

In summary, despite some measure of subscriber growth, CATV, once considered a "revolutionary" medium, remains a minor service in the American television system.

CONCLUSION

This analysis of cable television began by considering the problems that this service has experienced in getting on the Commission's agenda of significant concerns. CATV's early development as a service that was used merely to enhance the quality of television broadcast signals in outlying areas is important here. It contributed to the early view of cable as a minor feature of the broadcasting market. In addition to this, since the Commission was deeply involved in attempting to establish a workable broadcast allocation plan, cable could easily be looked upon as a temporary service until such problems were solved. The Commission was not in a position to reevaluate years of work and investment in broadcasting in order to consider another system of television. Making a reevaluation all the more remote a possibility was the uniqueness of CATV: it could neither be fit into the major categories of the Communications Act (broadcasting and common carrier) nor into the concept of a localized television system. Consequently, the Commission's sole concern about CATV in the early years of its development was whether it would pose interference or economic problems for the broadcast service.

This concern about the impact of CATV on television broadcasting continued into the latter 1950s but, with little evidence of direct harm, much uncertainty about the Commission's jurisdiction over CATV, and little pressure from major broadcasting interests, no action was taken until the next decade. In fact, in the early 1960s the Commission did not directly control cable systems, but simply used the stopgap measure of regulating the microwave companies that served cable systems.

There are a number of interesting factors connected with the FCC's direct regulation of cable which began in the latter half of the 1960s. First, the Commission avoided action until it was fairly clear that control measures would not be forthcoming from either the Congress or the judiciary. Second, the Commission's decision-making was influenced by the expressed need to avoid day-to-day regulation of CATV. Third, the Commission acted despite the recognition that it did not have the regulatory tools to determine with certainty whether CATV would actually have a negative impact on broadcast television. With a logic reminiscent of the FM case, the Commission majority argued that unless it could be assured that cable would not compete with broadcast television, it would strictly regulate CATV to prevent any harm to the broadcasting service. Thus, rather than consider the contribution that cable might make to the mass communications system, including one characterized by localism, the FCC majority focused solely on the potential negative impact of CATV. Finally, this decision-making was also characterized by a common Commission technique—the splitting of services between short and long-run possibilities, with CATV considered the future dominant television system.

While it is clear that there has been a good deal of pressure from the broadcasting industry to control cable growth, it is also true that there have been significant splits within both the cable and broadcast industries. The cable industry had been split between small operators who posed little threat to broadcast television, and larger systems that sought to grow into major markets through the importation of distant signals. Among the latter were several cable operators who sought out FCC regulation to avoid the complexities of state and local regulation. It is also important to recognize that it was not until the late 1960s that major broadcasters began to pressure the FCC to restrict cable. What is perhaps of greater significance is that many broadcasters (particularly during the cable "freeze") began to buy into cable systems. Today, over one-third of all systems are owned by broadcasters.

Here again, just as with FM and UHF, the responsibility for deciding the fate of a major broadcast market innovation was left with the FCC—an agency with the legal authority to decide, but with minimal support and inadequate resources. Just as in the other cases, such a situation led to conservative decision-making: Why risk upsetting the structure of established broadcasting by supporting a major competitor that may fail? The Commission would be the focus of blame for any harm that might come to the established system. Instead, it took the path of little risk—permit the innovation to survive—but only as a supplement to the dominant service. The next chapter reports on *another* potential "revolutionary" innovation that also became a secondary service.

8
Subscription Television: Challenge to "Free" TV

INTRODUCTION

This statement, applicable to many broadcasting innovations, refers to subscription television or "Pay-TV" as it is popularly known. It is a service that transmits television programs to viewers on an individual demand basis, i.e., viewers are charged for each program they select. To this date, there has been far more political wrangling than viewer selection.

Proposals for a subscription system date from as early as 1931 when Eugene F. MacDonald, founder of the Zenith Radio Corporation, proposed such a system for radio. MacDonald pioneered the development of a subscription television service at Zenith in the 1940s. After many years of delay and disagreement among government and industry interests, commercial experimentation began in Hartford, Connecticut, in 1962. Following the completion of these tests, the FCC issued its *Fourth Report and Order* (U.S. FCC, 1968a) establishing guidelines, consisting primarily of restrictions, for the operation of subscription television.

Research on STV has dealt primarily with different claims about what an STV service can actually offer. In an article frequently cited by proponents of subscription television, Jora Minasian (1964) contended that STV would both increase the diversity of programming and, perhaps more importantly, serve as a more exact barometer of public demand than the advertiser-supported system dominated by the controversial Nielsen rating system. According to him:

---

[1]Cited in Minow (1964, p. 231).

> In an advertiser supported system . . . the program results reflect an all-or-nothing type of voting since votes take weights of either one (viewer) or zero (nonviewer). In contrast, a subscription system allows proportional representation, since votes take different weights (different prices paid for different kinds of programs) and reveal the voter's subjective evaluation of the program.   (p. 75)

He concludes that greater diversity would result from the subscription system because it enables viewers to concentrate their "dollar votes" and overcome the relative unpopularity of their tastes. On the other hand, Noll and his colleagues (1973, p. 133) claim that such diversity would not be readily forthcoming because so-called minority programming would have to be very expensive to generate the same revenue as mass programming. They cite the example of a popular show which might draw 15 million viewers paying 10 cents per household and thus gross $1.5 million; for a minority program with approximately 1 million viewers, the price would have to be set at $1.50 per household in order to realize the same revenue as the mass appeal program (cf. Coase & Barrett, 1968, pp. 43, 64).

Other critics of STV have stressed that it would force people to pay for programming already received on the "free" system.[2] Some critics simply ignore the fact that buried in the "free" system are higher prices of products advertised on TV to cover ad costs; while others acknowledge that higher prices affect nonviewers (disproportionately higher income people) as well as viewers—with the latter receiving programs subsidized by those who can better afford to pay. In addition, the critics argue that because of the large revenues expected to be generated by viewer payments, STV companies would attract, or as it is commonly termed "siphon," the most popular talent from the established television service. Some considered this to be a particularly heavy blow to low income people who depend on television for news and entertainment to a greater extent than any other income class (Lees & Yang, 1966). Never before have network executives been such staunch supporters of poor people as they have been in the debate over subscription television.

Much of the research on the regulation of subscription television has focused on the efforts of major commercial broadcasters and movie theatre interests to exert pressure on the FCC to limit STV development. Most analysts have claimed that these efforts have met with considerable success. According to Borchardt (1970), "the commission rules (in 1968) sought to protect advertiser-supported commercial TV by prohibiting pay-TV operators from showing those sport, film, and series type programs which constitute the main programs of the former" (p. 71). R.H. Coase, a conservative proponent of subscription systems, has been more explicit. He contends (see Coase &

---

[2]This was noted particularly (and not unexpectedly) by Harry Olsson, General Counsel at CBS, and by Brenda Fox, a lawyer with the National Association of Broadcasters, in interviews with me, conducted in March 1975.

Barrett), that ". . . the reason for the lack of development is that the commercial broadcasting industry and the owners of movie theatres have been successful in exerting sufficient political pressure to prevent the emergence of a pay-TV system" (p. 17). This argument also receives the support of many of those who claim that even if STV were to develop free from external pressure, it would tend to mirror the current system of mass entertainment because minority programing would not be profitable enough to support the system (Noll et al., 1973, pp. 147–49).

GETTING ON THE AGENDA

Once again, as with other broadcasting innovations, a notable characteristic in the development of STV was the amount of time that it took for the service to be considered as an item worthy of serious FCC attention. Organizational pressures and other factors contributed to this delay.

As was mentioned earlier, the concept of viewer payments for individual programs was initially suggested by Eugene MacDonald of Zenith in 1931 as a possible source of financing the radio broadcasting system without advertising. That such a system was suggested by MacDonald, considered a maverick like FM pioneer Edwin Armstrong, may help to explain why little serious attention was paid to the suggestion at this time.[3]

The first formal proposal for a subscription television service was made by Zenith in 1947 with its Phonevision system. It was three years before Zenith received FCC authorization to test the system in the Chicago area. Even then, the Commission limited such experimentation to the showing of movies that had been released for more than two years (U.S. FCC, *Annual Report: 1950*, p. 11; Minow, 1964, p. 231).

After two years of testing, Zenith sought approval for commercial development of an STV operation from the FCC in 1952. At this time, however, subscription television was a minor concern of the Commission and its staff, mired as they were in the complexities of attempting to establish a national television broadcasting system after a four-year freeze on station allocations. In addition to this and somewhat reminiscent of the cable television case, the Commission (U.S. FCC, *Annual Report: 1953*, p. 98) was in a quandary over whether to consider STV as a broadcasting or common carrier service. Furthermore, it questioned the usefulness of reserving a portion of already scarce spectrum space for the new service. It is interesting that the Commission made no positive connection between subscription television and the already troubled UHF service. Could not the reservation of several of the

[3]This interpretation was suggested by Hyman Goldin in an interview with me in December 1974.

many UHF channels for STV development also provide a much needed impetus to the development of the former? There was no consideration of this possibility and a proposed rulemaking on STV was delayed until 1955.

ON THE AGENDA

In February of 1955, the Commission issued a *Notice of Proposed Rule Making* seeking petitions on the merits of establishing a commercial STV system. Specifically, the Commission (U.S. FCC, *Annual Report: 1955*) considered it necessary to establish ". . . what safeguards are necessary to insure that the public would continue to receive well-balanced TV programming without charge" (p. 98). Thus, even before any campaign was mounted by the broadcasting industry and the Congress, the Commission's chief concern was to safeguard the "standard broadcast" or "free TV" service.

The response to the Commission request for filings was somewhat extraordinary. According to the Commission report: "Filings in this connection have been more voluminous than in any previous docket case in the Commission's history, with more than 25,000 formal documents, letters, postcards, etc., filling nearly 70 reference volumes" (p. 98). Inundated with filings, the Commission (U.S. FCC, 1957b) further delayed its rule-making on STV. It claimed that ". . . it is not possible for us to make sound determinations concerning the classification of the proposed service, or to reach well-founded conclusions concerning its political impact on the public and on the established system of broadcasting on the basis of information so far" (p. 3759).

While the Commission delayed a final determination, it both asserted jurisdiction over STV (U.S. FCC, 1957a, p. 1509) and began to treat the service as it had other innovations—as ancillary to the established broadcasting system. This latter point is particularly interesting when considering a statement contained in a 1956 (U.S. FCC, *Annual Report*) Commission report. In it the Commission noted that: "Concentration on TV's general difficulties precluded Commission attention to some other weighty broadcast problems, such as subscription TV, TV community antennas, and the AM 'clear channel' and 'daytime skywave' proceedings" (p. 8). No mention is made of the possibility that certain of those "weighty problems," like subscription television, might actually help to deal with television's "general difficulties."

In October, 1957, the Commission issued its *First Report* on subscription television (U.S. FCC, 1957a). The major feature of the report was a decision to accept applications for STV market tests. Initially, the FCC agreed to allow any system to be tested in up to three markets, and more than one system to be tried out in a single market. The Commission limited test markets to those that were already served by at least three other commercial television stations. Thus, no tests would be allowed in those markets where STV might be particularly helpful, that is, those areas that had failed to attract more than two broadcasting stations. The Commission would thus maximize the competitive opposition to STV, while minimizing the potential harm to local broadcasting outlets.

The Commerce Committee in the House of Representatives did not concur at all with this interpretation. Leading the anti-STV forces, Chairman Oren Harris (cited in Cary, 1967) claimed that ". . . the scope of the tests contemplated by the Commission in its first report was so broad there was grave risk that these tests would bring about the virtual establishment of a new subscription television service on some extended or permanent basis" (p. 48). The House Committee formally opposed the trial authorization in a "sense of the Commitee" resolution (Pike and Fisher, *Radio Regulation,* 16, p. 153a). The FCC responded to this action with its *Second Report* on STV by agreeing to delay the trial authorization until after the 85th Congress adjourned.

In its *Third Report* on STV, issued in 1959, the Commission responded to Congressional pressure by severely curtailing the initial test conditions. A particular STV system could now only be tested in one market, and only one system could be authoritzed for any market with three or more conventional television stations. In addition, the Commission prohibited STV proprietors from selling to the public any more equipment than was necessary for the reception of "free" broadcasts (U.S. Congress, House, 1967, pp. 4–5). The Senate Commerce Committee approved these further limitations by a narrow 11 to 10 margin (Pike and Fisher, *Radio Regulation,* 16, p. 1540). Several Senators were opposed to merely testing a subscription service.

The result was that, rather than having competing systems tested in the same market and individual systems in different markets, the actual "trial" conditions were limited to one system (Zenith–Teco) in one market (Hartford, Connecticut). Given the pressure from Congressional, broadcasting, and movie theatre interests, as well as the complexity of the Commission's other concerns, it is not difficult to understand why the FCC did not seriously consider subscription television as a service with significant potential. From the final result—one system tested in one market—it appears that it was more important to the Commission that a test be taken than what the test could actually show. The symbolic value seems to have been a more important consideration than the informational value. With STV considered apart from other services, the Commission would appear to have covered its STV responsibilities; even though to generalize from this single market test on the feasibility of establishing a subscription service throughout the many diverse markets in the country would be little better than guesswork, if not worse. It was not until 1968 that the Commission publicly recognized that little was learned from the Hartford tests that could be applied on a national scale (U.S. FCC, 1968a, pp. 495 ff.).

Subscription television entrepreneurs encountered additional problems in attempting to establish test systems in markets other than Hartford. In a development exemplifying the power of motion picture and broadcasting interests to mount a strong campaign against subscription television, California voters approved a 1964 referendum preventing the establishment of an STV system in the state.[4] Even though the election results were eventually overturned by the California Supreme Court,[5] the sponsors of an STV system in the state gave up on the project.

In addition to this, Zenith's attempts in 1965 to expand its Hartford tests to a greater number of markets and to expand the programming for a greater part of the day were rejected by the Commission (U.S. FCC, *Annual Report: 1965*, pp. 114–15). In the next year, Zenith proposed the establishment of a nationwide commercial STV system; the Commission responded in March of that year with another *Notice of Proposed Rulemaking* requesting further comments.

As part of this extended information-gathering process, the FCC established an internal Committee on Subscription Television which issued a 1967 report in support of setting up a restricted national system.[6] (U.S. FCC, *Annual Report: 1967,* p. 39). Nevertheless, Commission Chairman Rosel Hyde continued to argue before the House Commerce Committee (U.S. Congress, House, 1967) that, despite the many years of testimony and study, the FCC was still undecided on subscription television:

> In sum, this proceeding has been formally pending for more than 12 years. . . . I want to stress that the Commission has reached no decision on this question. In conclusion, may I emphasize again that there has been no resolution of the issues which have been argued so extensively before us. (p. 4)

It was not until 1968 that the Commission (U.S. FCC, 1968a) agreed to license subscription television systems for commercial operation. However, in order to protect what the Commission considered "free" television, the following major constraints were imposed on the development of STV:

1.   Subscription systems could operate only in markets that contained five or more commercial television stations including the STV outlet.

2.   Only one STV outlet would be licensed in each market.

3.   Limits were set on the type of programming permissible for use by STV operators: In general, most continous series and feature motion picture films as well as sporting events that have typically been aired over the past

---

[4]For a history of the California case see *Broadcasting,* September 2, 1964; November 9, 1964; May 24, 1965; and March 7, 1966.

[5]*Weaver v. Jordan,* 64 Cal. (2d) 235 (1966).

[6]Actually two of three Commissioners on the Committee supported the establishment of a system. Committee Chairman Wadsworth withheld judgment on the proposal but did agree that the issues should be brought before the full Commission membership.

two years on advertiser supported television could not be shown on STV.

4. STV stations were required to broadcast "conventional" television programming without charge to subscribers for a minimum of twenty-eight hours per week.

In addition, it was decided that the rules would not take effect for at least six months, ". . . to afford an opportunity for judicial and Congressional review of that action before the granting of any application for a particular STV service to a community" (U.S., Congress, House, 1969, p. 24).

In sum, STV systems were restricted to the most competitive markets that would be limited in the type of programming that could be shown and also required to offer an average of four hours of broadcasting per day free of charge. This would guarantee, according to a Commission report, "that STV will be a supplement and not a replacement for conventional free TV service" (U.S. FCC, *Annual Report: 1969,* p. 40).

According to the dissenting statement of Commissioner Bartley (U.S. FCC, June 24, 1970, Dissent), these rules would guarantee something else— "complete strangulation of a potentially new economic base for program origination." The dissent of Commissioner Loevinger was even stronger. He argued that "the program supervision proposed . . . is impractical, ill-advised, unwise, illegal, and unconstitutional and a few other things" (U.S. Congress, House, 1967, p. 382).

A milder, though perhaps more significant, basis of criticism was the apparent inconsistency in the Commission's rationale when compared to other areas of FCC policy-making. In other cases the Commission claimed that Section 307(b) of the Communications Act required it to distribute services equally throughout the country and therefore deprive no local area of service. As discussed earlier, this concept of localism was used to justify the 1952 VHF–UHF allocation policy against petitions for a regional service as well as to support the restriction of cable television systems. In the case of subscription television, however, the FCC limited STV to areas where there already were at least four other commercial stations. This was criticized by Zenith representatives (U.S. Congress, House, 1967) who contended that:

> The underlying policy of Section 307(b) of the Communications Act, which requires the Commission to make a fair, efficient, and equitable distribution of broadcast service among the several "communities," would appear to dictate that subscription television be made available in all markets. In short, if there is a demand for subscription service, the public in all markets is entitled to its benefits if someone is willing to supply it. (p. 350)

Opponents of subscription television also used this argument as a basis for criticizing the Commission's STV rules. Here, however, a concern for localism was linked to the problem of monopoly. For example, according to an ABC representative (U.S. Congress, House, 1967):

> . . . pay television would be made available principally in the larger urban areas of the

country. However well motivated, this would be discriminating and unfair to the less populated parts of the country.

In the interest of protecting free television from this impact of pay TV, the FCC also proposed to limit the number of franchises in any community to one; in doing so it would create monopolies. (p. 395)[7]

The Commission Report on STV deals with this criticism by stressing an overruling consideration (U.S. FCC, 1968a):

. . . we regard the continued availability of free programming as a most important consideration. Although we are aware of the merits of the arguments that STV in all communities might help marginal or new stations in small communities, might aid UHF in such communities, might promote diversity of programming; arguments that section 307(b) of the act requires that STV be allowed in all communities where a demand exists . . . where uncertainty about the new service exists with regard to this subject, considerations of protecting against preempting are overriding. (pp. 518–19)

As was noted earlier, the Commission had claimed for several years that it was important to protect small market and particularly UHF television outlets. Now that the Commission had a service which the majority of its members admitted might very well provide such assistance and, in addition, increase program diversity, the Commission restricted the operation of that service to those markets with the most television stations and the greatest amount of competition.

The Commission majority thus turned from a value that some have considered to be a most prominent one for the FCC—a localized television broadcasting service—largely in order to protect the established television system. It is clear that once STV came to the FCC's attention, it was considered not in terms of the contribution that it might make to the national television system, but rather as a threat to the Commission's conception of what should be dominant in that system. A Commission majority neither prevented STV from developing at all, nor did it give the service the freedom to compete with the existing television service. As in the other cases, the FCC avoided the potential conflict between the conventional television system and STV. However, the Commission did not categorize subscription television as a "long-run" possibility (as it had FM, UHF, and CATV), but rather in terms of "whether STV would provide a beneficial supplement to the program choices now available to the public" (U.S. FCC, 1968a, p. 473). Here, "beneficial supplement" replaces "the long run" as a justification for separating the innovation, in this case STV, from the established system.

This point has been another source of critical commentary on the *Fourth Report and Order*. For example, in hearings before the House Commerce Committee (U.S. Congress, House, 1967), a representative of the Americans for Democratic Action commented that:

---

[7]For similar comments by Vincent Wasilewski, President of the National Association of Broadcasters, see U.S. Congress, House (1969, p. 55).

ADA considers the basic premise of the Committee's (the FCC Committee on STV) Report to be fallacious. Educational programming was also first regarded as a 'beneficial supplement' to commercial broadcasting; . . . FM channels were regarded as beneficial supplements to AM. (p. 644)

One way to understand why it is that the FCC consistently resorts to this approach is to view the Commission as an organization that avoids conflicts inherent in the complexity of its tasks. It imposes a simplifying structure upon this complexity by considering the established system of television broadcasting, in the absence of "coercive facts," as primary, and the innovation is regarded as a "long-run" possibility or a "beneficial supplement." In this way Commissioners avoid the risk of committing themselves to what they referred to as the "uncertainty about the new service" (U.S. FCC, 1968a, p. 519).

It is interesting to note that STV opponents clearly understood this point. In fact, their opposition to STV may have been all the stronger because they recognized that once a service became part of the established television system, it would be almost impossible to remove it. For example, an ABC representative expressed concern in Congressional testimony because "Commission experience demonstrates the difficulty of 'turning the clock back' after interests become established, after the public has relied upon the Commission's action, and after substantial expenditures have been made." (U.S. Congress, House, 1967, p. 393). This concern was also aired by powerful members of Congress. Chairman Celler of the House Judiciary Commitee noted that once STV won Commission approval, it would only be a short time before pressure to lift all restrictions became so great that subscription television would dominate the television industry (U.S. Congress, House, 1967, p. 379).

This strongly felt concern leads us to consider an apparent contradiction in the views of many STV opponents. It is summarized well by one such opponent, Martin Gaines, General Counsel for the National Association of Theatre Owners and the Joint Committee Against Toll-TV: ". . . aren't people like myself a little bit inconsistent saying on the one hand there is no demand, on the other hand it is such a tremendous demand that it will destroy free television?" (U.S. Congress, House, 1967, pp. 548–49). Gaines answers his own question by claiming that there is no contradiction, because demand which does not exist today can be created by the STV industry, particularly if it caused the established television industry to decline. The only way for this to happen, however, would be if subscription television were able to attract substantial public support.

The inconsistency related to public demand is connected to several problems that are of central importance in considering the restrictive position taken by the Commission on this and other innovations in the broadcasting market. If the innovation is considered to be of minor significance, or one that would not elicit much demand, why regulate it as if it were a major threat to the established system? If the innovation is considered of major importance, or one that might be in great demand, why is it necessary to protect the established system from the innovation? Why not allow the innovation to compete as part of the "established" service rather than restrict it as a "long-term" possibility or as a "beneficial supplement?" Not only were these questions unanswered by the Commission, but they were not even raised as legitimate questions.[8]

The protection of an established system is made easier when interests representing that system are united in support of the Commission. There is no doubt that the three major networks were opposed to the development of STV. The testimony of an NBC representative clearly summarizes the network position (U.S. Congress, House, 1967):

> We think a system using broadcast frequencies to charge viewers for programs would narrow the base of broadcasting and violate the public interest in two respects: It requires set owners to pay for programs of the type they now enjoy free; in the process it would threaten the ability of free television to continue and expand its present services. (p. 185)[9]

Opposition was also strong from movie theatre interests represented by the National Association of Theatre Owners and the Joint Committee Against Toll-TV (U.S. Congress, House, 1967, pp. 416–17). In addition, members of Congress have introduced over 60 bills to amend the Communications Act and explicitly prohibit subscription television (Noll et. al., 1973, p. 129).

This opposition was no doubt a potent force influencing the Commission's ultimate decision. However, to understand it accurately, three further points need to be considered.

First, even before industry and Congressional concern was directed at this issue, the Commission, in 1953, formulated the framework in which it would evaluate STV, i.e., will it be a "proper supplement" or will it impair the development of "free-TV?" (U.S. FCC, *Annual Report: 1953*, p. 98). The message here is clear: From the first the Commission used what would become the industry–Congress question to judge STV.

Second, while there were very potent forces in the broadcasting industry opposed to STV, there were important exceptions—important particularly because they illuminate the Commission's real priorities in this case. While most VHF broadcasters opposed the development of STV, most UHF operators, represented by such organizations as the All-Channel Television Society, supported the licensing of subscription systems. The latter generally felt that the addition of STV programming would be a major help to this declining sector of the television industry. According to Martin Firestone, counsel for ACTS,

---

[8]One or more of these questions has sometimes been raised as part of dissenting opinions. See p. 95.

[9]For the comments of CBS and ABC spokespersons see U.S. Congress, House (1967, p. 663; 1969, p. 77).

". . . the authorization of such a system will, under proper regulatory conditions, aid in the economic development of marginal UHF stations in the larger
television markets, and will encourage the lighting up of presently dark UHF
allocations" (U.S. Congress, House, 1967, p. 619). Firestone defined "proper regulatory conditions" as those in which STV by cable (now called pay-
cable) would be prohibited because such systems would cut further into
dwindling UHF revenues (pp. 620–21). Firestone suggested that the Commission allow over-the-air subscription television to compete with the established
broadcasting system with only one constraint: To protect against excessive
program siphoning, deny license renewals to STV station operators who simply mirror the programming of established stations. In other words, Firestone
wanted the Commission to stimulate competition in the television industry and
make all stations live up to the content of their license applications.

Firestone's contention was supported by W. Robert McKinney, President of
UHF station WJRJ in Atlanta. McKinney claimed that he was continuing to
lose money in a market that contained three VHF stations affiliated with the
major networks. He argued that permission to use his UHF outlet for subscription television would certainly boost his station (pp. 654–61). That the Commission refused to act on his and similar pleas of UHF station owners was
evidence to him that the Commission's many supportive pronouncements on
UHF were little more than a cover for its real concern—the protection of network affiliated VHF stations.

A third important point for understanding the nature of pressure on the
Commission in this case is that much of the opposition was not directed at
establishing an STV service, but at what appeared to be the Commission's
direct involvement in program control—beyond the accepted areas of regulating questions of obscenity and political fairness. Recognizing the significance
of established precedents for the Commission, many broadcasters feared that
such control might now more readily be applied to them. This is made clear
in the December 16, 1968 issue of *Broadcasting* magazine that appeared
shortly after the Commission's 1968 rules on STV were made public. One
article attempts to explain why the opposition to subscription television was
on the wane: "It is simply because subscription television is not considered
the threat to free television it once was" (p. 42). Nevertheless, an editorial
appearing later on in the same issue claims that:

> In effect the FCC has voted 5 to 1 to suspend the First Amendment. . . . It is not neces-
> sary to take a position for or against pay TV to see the grave dangers of this FCC deci-
> sion. If the commission can make explicit choices of the kinds of programming pay TV
> may transmit, what is to stop it from making equally explicit choices in the programming
> on the existing commercial and noncommercial systems.

Thus, a major concern of broadcasters was the possibility that program control
would become more widespread given the limitations that the FCC was imposing on subscription television.

THE AFTERMATH: STV GOES NOWHERE

While there has been action in the courts and in Congress following adoption of the 1968 rules, little has taken place within the industry to suggest the development of a subscription television service, particularly one using broadcasting as opposed to cable.

In a suit brought against the FCC by the National Association of Theatre Owners and the Joint Committee Against Toll-TV, an Appeals Court determined in 1969 that the Commission acted within the legal limits of the Communications Act in setting STV rules.[10] This decision was made to stand in 1970 when the Supreme Court denied certiorari.[11]

Following the Commission's 1968 decision, 20 bills were introduced for consideration before the House Commerce Committee calling for a complete ban on subscription television. While a measure significantly increasing restrictions on STV did receive the support of a Committee majority, it failed to win full Congressional approval (*Broadcasting,* October 10, 1969, p. 30; May 4, 1970, p. 49).

Despite the inability of anti-STV forces to win an outright ban on the service, the FCC did incorporate a major component of the Commerce Committee's bill into its STV rules. The Commission extended from two to five years the period of time that a sporting event would have to be off the established television system before it could be shown on an STV outlet. This would prevent STV interests from purchasing the rights to a major sports event, keeping it off the air for two years and then showing it on a subscription basis. In addition, the FCC extended from two to ten years a prohibition on subscription programming of sporting events, such as the Olympic games that recur regularly at intervals of more than a year (U.S. FCC, *Annual Report: 1972,* p. 49).

That such further restrictions were necessary to protect the established system is doubtful. While some attempts have been made to launch a broadcast STV service, none have succeeded. (cf. *Broadcasting,* July 6, 1970; U.S. FCC, *Annual Report: 1971,* p. 38).[12] According to Kahn (1971), ". . . because of the restrictive terms under which the Commission's rules permit Pay-TV operations, it seems improbable that this mode of pay-as-you-see

---

[10]*National Association of Theatre Owners and Joint Committee Against Toll TV v. FCC,* 420 F(2d) 194 (1969).

[11]397 U.S. 922 (1970).

[12]Barry Zorthian, while Vice-President in charge of government relations for Time, Inc., indicated to me in a March 1975 interview that there is only one firm seriously considering an over-the-air STV operation. This is the Tel Ease Corporation owned by Robert S. Block who holds a UHF license in Milwaukee, Wisconsin. Zorthian who was in charge of Time's cable interests prior to their recent divestiture, said that the requirement that STV systems broadcast free for 28 hours a week makes it economically unfeasible for them to operate.

transmission could achieve substantial penetration unless it were associated with cable TV or domestic satellite distribution'' (p. 613). (Cf. Noll et al., 1973, p. 273.)

Subscription television is increasingly being linked with CATV in so-called ''pay-cable'' systems. In 1977 a CATV publication reported that there were over 225 such systems serving over 635,000 households (*Broadcasting Cable Sourcebook,* 1977, p. 5). Not surprisingly, such systems are increasingly coming under attack from broadcasting interests.[13] In March 1975 the Commission issued its *First Report and Order* on pay-cable. Except for modest liberalizing of the feature film guidelines, the Commission essentially applied the same restrictions to pay-cable that had been imposed on subscription broadcasting systems. While the Commission recognized that there was ''sparse'' evidence for retaining rules prohibiting pay telecasts of such programming as a continuous series, it nevertheless retained the full restrictions pending a further inquiry (U.S. FCC, 1975, p. 65). According to the Commission, this was necessary to insure that subscription programming maintain its ''supplemental role'' vis à vis the established television system (p. 43).

CONCLUSION

This has been an attempt to explain how the subscription television service has developed in ways comparable to other broadcast market innovations. It began with a consideration of the difficulty that subscription television had in getting on the Commission's agenda of significant broadcasting concerns. Such factors as the promotion of STV by Eugene MacDonald, a maverick in the broadcasting industry, and the difficulty that Commission members had in incorporating the service within the FCC's primary communications categories help to explain the long delay in STV development. Of course, that the period during which subscription television service was first proposed was also marked by the complexities of attempting to deal with the television ''freeze'' and the subsequent station allocation plan did not at all help the establishment of a subscription service. What was crucial to the latter was that from the time of the earliest Zenith proposal to develop STV, a majority of Commission members focused on the negative impact of such a service on the so-called ''free'' broadcast system. There was no consideration of STV's potential benefit—particularly for weak UHF outlets. As in the other cases, the services were separated, with STV considered from the start as an ancillary system at best.

When subscription television began to be considered seriously by the

---

[13]For statements by representatives of NAB, the Joint Committee Against Toll-TV, and the Association of Maximum Service Telecasters see U.S. Congress, House (1967, pp. 410, 467, 563–601).

Commission in the 1950s, action was further delayed by the record quantity of filings as well as by the pressure of Congressional, broadcasting, and movie theatre interests. The latter contributed to the severe limitation on STV testing, as well as to the highly restrictive rules that the Commission imposed on subscription systems in 1968. This Commission action is particularly interesting because a majority of members explicitly set aside any concerns for localism and UHF outlets in favor of strict controls that would protect the network dominated system. It also brought to the forefront the contradiction over consumer demand and regulation that is clearly applicable to other cases. Specifically, if one assumes that there is little demand for a service (as STV opponents argued), then why control it? On the other hand, if one foresees a large demand, then should not the potential value of promoting the service be given some consideration? Actual decision-making simply avoided such questions—the overriding criterion has been to protect whatever came first to dominance.

Subscription television certainly represents a challenge to "free TV." Thus far, the emphasis has been on characterizing the established service as free and therefore requiring protection. But, like other innovations, STV represents a challenge to free television from the control of a network system that profits by severely restricting the uses of the medium. This challenge has certainly been contained.

9
Summary: Four Decades, Four Innovations, Similar Results

THE OUTCOMES

In Chapter 2, I reported on the parallel between the growth of American broadcasting and the amount of criticism that has been directed at the system. Most of this analysis has dealt with one major reason why the parallel still exists—the control of innovations in the broadcasting market has contributed to the continued growth of the AM radio and VHF television systems, as well as to the continued criticism of the general lack of diversity in radio and television programming.

The dominance of AM radio operators, particularly the multiple station owners that run the most powerful urban operations, has been supported by the control of FM radio. Several FCC actions were central to the maintenance of that control, especially the shift in the initial spectrum area assigned to FM and the "single market plan" which reduced the maximum power of major metropolitan FM outlets. The Commission reinforced the control of FM by encouraging AM owners to acquire FM stations for program duplication and by continuing to permit AM station drop-ins into an admittedly overcrowded spectrum band.

The dominance of VHF television, particularly that of the three major networks, has been supported by the restriction of three innovations in the television market.

First to be controlled was UHF television. The FCC permitted VHF stations to develop despite its own recognition that technical limitations prohibited the sole use of VHF for a competitive national television system. Furthermore, VHF stations grew in value during the years of artificial scarcity created by the freeze on station licensing. As a result, stations developing in the more plentiful UHF spectrum area began commercial operation at a competitive disadvantage that was made all the more severe by a station allocation plan that forced UHF stations to compete directly with VHFs in the same community. The lack of Commission support for proposals to create some all-UHF markets, its encouragement of satellite stations that widened the audience of VHF outlets, its search for more VHF spectrum space, its continued attempts to squeeze in more VHF stations—all were important policies contributing to the growth of network-dominated VHF television at the expense of UHF.

The story has been repeated for cable television. The Commission viewed cable for several years as an inconsequential medium—merely an auxiliary service that might create interference problems for the established VHF system. This perspective continued to dominate the Commission's cable policy despite changes within the cable industry and its technology that enhanced CATV's potential for widening competition and increasing program diversity. In fact, it was these very changes that led to stricter Commission control over CATV. As CATV moved from simply a potential source of interference to an actual competitive threat to the established television system, the FCC moved to further restrict the service through such actions as its controls on the importation of distant broadcast signals into major CATV markets. These controls and others have helped maintain the ancillary status of CATV.

Subscription television was similarly hampered. Except for references to the need to protect the established "free" television system from the subscription service, the Commission rarely considered STV in the initial years after Zenith proposed the service. Commercial development of STV was delayed further until admittedly inadequate tests were conducted. Finally, when the FCC sanctioned commercial operation of a subscription service in 1968, STV was so severely restricted that no broadcast system has yet been able to grow. Similar rules have been applied to pay cable systems, though these operations have shown signs of potential growth.

THE INFLUENCES

This analysis has concentrated not only on elements in the outcomes of the four cases, but also on characteristic features of the decision-making processes that led to these outcomes. While this research has been concerned with the influence of complexity upon organizational decision-making, the result of this inquiry itself has been something of an exercise in complexity. For there does not appear to be one single key to understanding FCC decision-making.

Nevertheless, a perspective centering on complexity was particularly helpful in dealing with certain questions that other more commonly considered perspectives could not fully answer. Complexity was viewed broadly as a feature of problems characterized by a high degree of uncertainty not only about the information needed to find solutions, but also about the power to make decisions on these problems.

Complexity functions as a major constraint on organizational activity that is particularly significant when decision-makers are faced with innovative challenges to an established system. Innovations provide excellent opportunities to study complex decision problems because they are typically embedded in a context of significant uncertainty. They create a situation in which organizational decision-makers must determine whether to risk investing their resources in the innnovation and pay the political costs that may be associated with the decline of the established system, even when they are uncertain about whether or not the innovation will succeed. The costs become that much greater when it is a regulatory agency like the FCC that is faced with the innovative challenge. For an organization like the FCC stands to benefit less than a business corporation from investing in an innovation. The regulatory agency stands to lose much by promoting the development of an innovation that simply does not perform as expected. The regulatory decision-maker is not involved with seeking to gain an edge in the market, but more typically with maintaining a stable service.

The cognitive perspective is useful for understanding the response of the FCC to the complexities of each innovative challenge. These features of this perspective are especially valuable:

1. Commission decision-makers typically responded to complexity by imposing a structure on it rather than use any sort of probablistic judgments. This structure appears to relieve the uncertainty created by these innovations. The structure itself is derived from a conception of the broadcasting system centered on AM radio and VHF television. That these two were the major elements of the structure can be traced to these factors:

a. AM radio and VHF television were the first to develop in their respective areas and therefore the first to receive heavy industry and public investments.

b. Each was supported by a significant power within the broadcasting industry—generally RCA. This is particularly important in light of the Commission's need to turn to industry representatives for expert assistance.

2. The Commission generally ignored information that did not conform to its conception of what ought to be dominant in the radio and television system. Rather than constantly reevaluating a set of priorities in the light of new data, Commission members simply avoided the potential uncertainty inherent in such new information. This helps explain why it took so long for each innovation to become an item to warrant serious Commission attention despite the information made available to Commission members that indicated how each innovation could help solve problems that members themselves considered to be significant. Thus, it took several years for FM radio to be taken seriously by the Commission despite concerns expressed repeatedly in its reports about the problems of a maldistribution of service and the increasing concentration of power in the hands of a few major companies. It took several

years for UHF television to be considered seriously despite Commission ex-
pressions of concern for the inadequacy of the VHF service. In fàct, it was
not until the Commission was faced with the severe coercive fact represented
by the technical problems of the crowded VHF area that UHF was given more
than passing FCC consideration for commercial development. A lengthy
period of time passed before CATV was regarded as a major agenda item,
and this was not until other organizations such as the Congress and the courts
chose not to restrict cable development. Finally, a decade passed before the
Commission turned its attention to subscription television which, like CATV,
was regarded as a potential boost to the development of UHF television and a
source of program diversity. It appears that a tradeoff was made: Commission
decision-makers gained the ability to act explicitly in the fact of complexity,
as they closed out new sources of information. They essentially avoided complexity by operating within the confines of a simplified cognitive structure.

3.   The Commission further avoided conflicts among services by separating them within distinct categories. For example, when the problem of
monopoly was viewed as a significant flaw in the AM radio service, FM was
not used to deal with the problem. Rather, the Commission restricted the development of FM in order to prevent a similar problem from occurring in that
service. This exacerbated the problem of monopoly, not only in the AM service, but in all of radio, because FM was so restricted that it failed to grow.
The Commission then encouraged AM station owners to bail out the declining
FM service by purchasing FM stations. Similarly, UHF, CATV, and STV
were all viewed as separate and antagonistic services rather than as potential
contributors to each other's development and to a generally more expansive
television system.

Perhaps more importantly, at different times over the course of three decades, FM, UHF, and CATV were considered the *long-run* solutions to problems in the broadcasting system. In fact, each was referred to in Commission
reports as the future dominant service in either radio or television. However,
at the same time, each innovation was further restricted by the promotion of
the established AM radio or VHF television system "for the short run."
While the Commission has never discussed shifting all television to a subscription service, STV was set aside from the established service as a "beneficial supplement" to it.

It is important to recognize that in no case was an innovation completely
prevented from developing. Each was, and continues to be, viewed as ancillary to the dominant service. In this way the Commission avoids the uncertainties and hence the risks of promoting innovations into a primary position,
while at the same time retaining them as future possibilities.

Particular attention was directed to a perspective based on complexity, because of its usefulness and because it has been rarely considered in organizational analyses. Most research on the FCC has focused on such factors as the

local service concept, the Commission staff, and relationships with other organizations. All of these areas could not be extensively explored in this report. Nevertheless, a consideration of these forces proved helpful in specific instances for understanding both how AM and VHF came to be considered as the primary components of broadcasting, as well as how they were maintained in that position. For example, the declining fortunes of the four innovations analyzed here have been traced, in part, to the potent opposition of particular industry interests.

Such factors as the above need to be specified more carefully than they have been in the literature on these cases. For example, in each case there have been significant differences within the industry. In the FM case, there was a split between RCA and CBS that was connected to another split between these two major industry forces in the television station allocation case. Aside from pointing to how different innovations are interconnected, it indicates that it is overly simplistic to view the FCC as simply "captured" by the established industry. A similar situation was indicated in the CATV and STV cases. In the former, it was noted that over one-third of all systems are now owned by broadcasting organizations—obviously weakening the impetus for general broadcast industry pressure to control cable. While the forces supporting subscription television have not been as potent, they did generally include backers of UHF television. In the face of this confusing complex of shifting interests, the most important point to keep in mind is that the Commission does not have to be explicitly "captured": The decision-making process is so structured that certain major industry interests get what they want without having to apply pressure directly.

The report did not view other constraints such as the local service doctrine and staff pressure as comparably significant. It was noted how localism, while of some significance in the UHF case, was a rather weak force, when it was not totally disregarded, in the more recent rulings on CATV and subscription television. In addition, while staff concerns were particularly significant in such decisions as the FM spectrum shift, staff interests have just as frequently lost out, particularly in the more recent CATV and STV cases.

This report has provided the basis for comparing decision-making activities in the important area of government regulation of business activity. That several common grounds were found for comparing four cases in the area of broadcast regulation is encouraging, particularly when it is considered that these cases have spanned four decades of broadcasting history, encompassing nearly the entire history of the FCC and including five Democratic and three Republican Presidential administrations. Table 9.1 is particularly illustrative in this regard. As the chart clearly indicates, there has been a heavy turnover in Commission membership as well as an even distribution of political party affiliation in the years covered by these cases.

Thus, despite the span of time and changes in Commission personnel, there are important similarities that have characterized the way in which the FCC has dealt with four innovations in the broadcasting market, as well as important parallels in the outcomes of these cases. The next chapter deals with the implications of these findings.

TABLE 9.1
FCC Commissioners, 1934–1977[a]

Commissioners	Party affiliation	Years of service
Eugene O. Sykes[b]	Democrat	1934–1939
Thad H. Brown	Republican	1934–1940
Paul A. Walker[b]	Democrat	1934–1953
Norman C. Case	Republican	1934–1945
Irvin Stewart	Democrat	1934–1937
George Henry Payne	Republican	1934–1943
Hampson Gary	Democrat	1934–1935
Anning S. Prall[b]	Democrat	1935–1937
T. A. M. Craven	Democrat	1937–1944
Frank M. McNinch[b]	Democrat	1937–1939
Frederic I. Thompson	Democrat	1939–1941
James Lawrence Fly[b]	Democrat	1939–1944
Ray C. Wakefield	Republican	1941–1947
Clifford J. Durr	Democrat	1941–1948
Ewell K. Jett[b]	Independent	1944–1947
Paul A. Porter[b]	Democrat	1944–1946
Charles R. Denny[b]	Democrat	1945–1947
William H. Wills	Republican	1945–1946
Rosel H. Hyde[b]	Republican	1946–1969
Edward M. Webster	Independent	1947–1956
Robert F. Jones	Republican	1947–1952
Wayne Coy[b]	Democrat	1947–1952
George E. Sterling	Republican	1948–1954
Frieda B. Hennock	Democrat	1948–1955
Robert T. Bartley	Democrat	1952–1972
Eugene H. Merrill	Democrat	1952–1953
John C. Doerfer[b]	Republican	1953–1960
Robert E. Lee	Republican	1953–
George C. McConnaughey[b]	Republican	1954–1957
Richard A. Mack	Democrat	1955–1958
T. A. M. Craven	Democrat	1956–1963
Frederick W. Ford[b]	Republican	1957–1964
John S. Cross	Democrat	1958–1962
Charles S. King	Republican	1960–1961
Newton W. Minow[b]	Democrat	1961–1963
William Henry[b]	Democrat	1962–1966
Kenneth A. Cox	Democrat	1963–1970
Lee Loevinger	Democrat	1963–1968
James J. Wadsworth	Republican	1965–1969

Commissioners	Party affiliation	Years of service
Nicholas Johnson	Democrat	1966–1973
H. Rex Lee	Democrat	1968–1974
Dean Burch[b]	Republican	1969–1974
Robert Wells	Republican	1969–1971
Thomas J. Houser	Republican	1971–1971 (Jan.–Oct.)
Charlotte T. Reid	Republican	1971–1977
Richard E. Wiley[b]	Republican	1972–1977
Benjamin L. Hooks	Democrat	1972–1977
James H. Quello	Democrat	1974–
Glen O. Robinson	Democrat	1974–1976
Abbott Washburn	Republican	1974–
Margita E. White	Republican	1976–
Joseph B. Fogarty	Democrat	1976–
Charles Ferris[b]	Democrat	1977–
Tyrone Brown	Democrat	1977–

[a]Source: U.S. FCC, *Annual Report: 1972*, p. 125, *Reports* through November, 1977.
[b]Indicates Chairman at some time during FCC tenure.

10
Implications

Many proposals have been offered to change the broadcasting system in America. This report has focused on the still unfulfilled hopes of those who looked to innovations in the system as the proposed cure—whether through the use of different frequencies such as FM in radio and UHF in television, new transmission facilities as with CATV, or new financing arrangements such as STV. While these innovations certainly do not cover the full range of possibilities, their common fate and that of the many other reform proposals listed in Table 1.1 strongly suggest that the structure of broadcasting in America, in operation now for five decades, is so deeply entrenched that changing it to make it more responsive to public needs, more open to the expression and control of more people, is certainly no easy task. But, one might ask, if the system has been so thoroughly criticized, why does it continue in its present form? More concretely, if everyone is dissatisfied with the system of broadcast regulation, so dissatisfied with the job that the FCC is doing, why does it continue? The critical point to understand here is that those who have been most strident in their criticism do not have the power to act on it; while those with the power have benefited and continue to benefit from the system's structure including the form of regulation centered on the FCC. Again, more concretely, those who own the broadcasting networks have profited economically from the oligopolistic nature of the system, while the FCC has served to absorb much of the criticism directed at the system. This is not to say that decision-makers at the FCC have simply sought to speak for established broadcasting interests. The problem is more structural than motivational: saddled with the responsibility for representing "the public interest" in the face of a huge industry whose resources far outstrip what the FCC is given, charged with acting on issues whose complexity often borders on the incredible, the FCC has typically avoided taking risks that might disrupt whatever service exists by viewing all new services in the context of that existing system. It is clear that without significant change, the system will continue as it is for a long time.

What options exist for changing the system? This report offers no simple blueprint for change, but rather suggests a number of alternatives derived from the findings.

COMPLETE REVIEW OF THE COMMUNICATIONS ACT

Over the past forty years recommendations for change have essentially involved tinkering with the basic legislation that solidified the structure of broadcast regulation in America—the 1934 Communications Act. The history of broadcasting teaches that no fundamental changes have come from such suggestions, and a complete review of the Act is long overdue. It is encouraging that the House Commerce Committee has recently begun to undertake the first such review of the Act.[1] It is important that public pressure be brought to bear on the Committee to see that this review produce more than a replication of the existing structure.

What should guide such a systematic review of the Act? There are primarily two prevailing views that apply chiefly to the broadcasting sphere: the need to insulate the Commission from external pressure, and the need to build the FCC's analytical and planning capability.

INSULATION FROM EXTERNAL PRESSURE

Several recent proposals have been based on the need to prevent the Commission from what former Commission General Counsel Henry Geller calls over-identification with powerful elements of the industry regulated (Geller, 1975, p. 706). Geller's proposal for corrective action is typical among these and includes the following suggestions to limit the possibility of industry influence:

1. Appoint Commissioners to 15-year terms at high salaries.

2. Bar reappointment to the Commission after the 15-year period but grant substantial pensions.

3. Bar employment in the communications field for a 10-year period following FCC service (pp. 722–723).

The evidence in this report clearly points to the need to restrict the influ-

---

[1] It is interesting that the review has been stimulated in part by AT&T's concern over the growth of competition in the common carrier area. That an earlier version of this report also helped stimulate the process is personally encouraging.

ence of established interests over the Commission. This should certainly be a major consideration in any general review of the Act. However, this report also raises questions about the specific remedies offered by Geller and others. For example, while extending the tenure of FCC members might insulate them from industry pressure, it would also give Commissioners more time to become committed to established broadcasting services and therefore, perhaps, be less open to innovations. If a consistent problem with the Commission is its tendency to evaluate innovations by viewing them within the structure of the historically established radio and television systems, then extending the tenure of Commissioners might very well exacerbate the problem.

Perhaps a more significant problem with such proposals is that they tend to focus on the direct relationship of the industry with the FCC. The evidence suggests, however, that a considerable amount of industry influence is exerted not directly on the Commission but through the Congress by the control that broadcasters have over the access of representatives to their constituencies. Any proposal to insulate the Commission from excessive industry influence would therefore have to deal with the complex of relationships in which the Commission is embedded, particularly that linking the industry to the Commission through Congress.

DEVELOP AN EFFICIENT ANALYSIS
AND PLANNING CAPABILITY

Another set of proposals traces the restriction of innovation to the Commission's failure to analyze problems comprehensively and develop specific policies for the long-term growth of communications systems. For example, FCC decision-making on cable television has been criticized because the Commission has been insensitive to economic research on such topics as the growth potential of CATV.

Starting from this view, several different policy proposals have been suggested:

—shift most of the Commission's administrative work to the Executive Branch and assign the FCC's judicial functions to the courts (Cushman, 1941; Minow, 1964; Special Committee on Administrative Law, 1934; U.S. Commission on Organization of Executive Bramch, 1949);

—reduce the Commission's size from seven members to a number that varies from five to a single administrator (Geller, 1975; President's Advisory Council, 1971; U.S. Congress, House, 1975);

—form strong departments within the Commission specifically charged with gathering information and using it to establish long-range communications policies (Attorney General's Committee on Administrative Procedure, 1941; Booz, et al., 1962; Committee for Economic Development, 1975; Emery, 1971; Park, 1973).

Again these proposals illuminate an area where major changes are necessary. However, the specific suggestions should be considered in light of the following questions raised by this report:

1. Those suggesting shifting most of the Commission's work to the Executive Branch contend that it would facilitate the planning and establishment of a unified government policy in the communications field. A cabinet level organization, it is surmised, would have more technical and political support to draw on than does an independent Commission. Nevertheless, experience with the executive-created Office of Telecommunications Policy suggests that the agency did develop the technical expertise to raise questions about the broadcasting system and its future direction that are rarely considered by the Commission. Nevertheless, OTP also involved itself in program content issues that primarily reflected the views of the administration in power. These involvements have overshadowed and severely curtailed the opportunity for OTP to serve as a source of general questioning and long-range planning for the Commission, and call into question the advisability of shifting broadcast regulatory authority to the Executive Branch.

2. Decreasing the Commission's size might help it to organize its efforts, including those directed at planning. However, such an action might also restrict the diversity of opinion of the Commission. Since a major problem with the FCC is the tendency to view innovations almost solely as threats to the established system, perhaps it would be beneficial to allow a greater number of alternative voices to be heard on the Commission itself.

3. Some claim that increasing the capacity of the Commission's staff to search for and process information could contribute to the planning effort. Such a proposal assumes that increasing the amount of information and speculation about alternatives in the broadcasting market is sufficient to induce Commissioners to consider innovations as other than intrinsically ancillary to established services. However, evidence suggests that Commission members are typically constrained by the complexity of their daily concerns, by a complexity that they order by imposing a simplifying structure derived from the established system. Because of this, information and speculation come to be considered merely as excess variety and the potential source of new uncertainties. They therefore tend to be ignored by Commission members in their decision-making.

EXPAND DIVERSITY

Some proposals would expand the amount of diversity in the decision-making process to make it more responsive to innovations. A number of options in this direction have been suggested:

—expand the role of the Executive, not to the point of taking full responsibility for regulation, but primarily to provide the Commission with a better policy planning capability (Landis, 1960; Noll, 1971b);

—increase consumer input to the decision-making process through such instruments as Nicholas Johnson's National Citizens Commission for Broadcasting (Johnson, 1970);

—recognize the reality that regulation is a political process, that regulatory bodies are "independent" in name only, by assigning positions on regulatory agencies to the representatives of specific interests (Noll, 1971b).

Evidence suggests that while it would be beneficial to increase diversity at the level of information-gathering, for such proposals to facilitate the consideration of innovations it would be necessary to increase diversity at the level of actual decision-making. Should the number of Commissioners be increased? Would it be possible to do so without making it more difficult to reach decisions? Is it possible to reserve positions on the Commission in such a way as to actually represent the diversity of interests in the communications field? Can this be done without locking positions into a number of substantive categories that might restrict future innovations? In other words, can we facilitate an openness in the decision-making *process,* without locking regulation into a consideration of a specific range of *outcomes?*

SYSTEMATIC REVIEW

Another set of alternatives begins with evidence suggesting that an environment characterized by rapid change and complexity restricts the long-term effectiveness of any specific organizational form. Research in very diverse historical settings illustrates how specific organizational forms, established to solve particular problems, eventually create significant problems of their own (Chandler, 1962; Udy, 1970; Schurmann, 1971). Proposals to deal with this include establishing a systematic review of regulatory agencies at fixed intervals, perhaps stimulated by legislation limiting the life span of each regulatory body (Friendly, 1962). Such so-called "sunset laws" are beginning to attract attention and may be one way to counteract the consistent pattern of treating innovations as intrinsically ancillary to the established system.

"IMMODEST" ALTERNATIVES

But are these proposals, any of them, strong enough remedies for the broadcasting system? Is it in need of some stronger, less modest, change? Whatever the answer to these questions, it is *at least* important to begin seriously considering more significant structural revisions. Such alternatives would range from deregulation of broadcasting to nationalization of the system. The former has been given some attention by economists who find it difficult to justify the existence of a commercial system that operates outside of normal market mechanisms, i.e., the system suffers because it is based on a government supported cartel. Proposals based on this perspective typically start from selling licenses for commercial broadcasting stations to the highest bidder (Coase, 1959; Levin, 1960, p. 175; U.S. Congress, House, 1958a, p. 160). It is felt that this would alleviate bureaucratic entanglements and raise a considerable amount of revenue. In 1969 the President's Office of Telecommunications Management issued a report claiming that deregulation would be particularly beneficial for innovations since regulation alone is

> not enough to bring about the introduction and use of equipment designed to higher standards to conserve spectrum space or to make extensive changes to benefit another user in the interests of efficient use of the spectrum. . . . Regulatory pressure will never match the rewards that could come from self-motivated research stimulated by direct economic benefit. (p. A-9)

Of course, deregulation alone would not guarantee a diversified media system free from monopoly concentration.

Not surprisingly, the issue of nationalization is not one that has been studied much, or, for that matter, frequently raised. Noll reports from a recent conference on regulation that some support did exist for government control in order to cure the "schizophrenia" over profits and the public interest (Noll, 1971b, pp. 14, 109). However, "Most of the conferees on both sides of the nationalization issue recognized that their views on the matter were largely instinctive. Little evidence has been gathered for or against government ownership" (p. 109). It is time that more attention be paid to this alternative, if only to advance discussion beyond the instinctive reaction level. Perhaps, to be successful, proposals to change the broadcasting system in America need to parallel the profits of the broadcasting networks—in their immodesty.

Appendix. Chronology of Relevant Events

1887   Interstate Commerce Act establishes the first independent regulatory agency, the Interstate Commerce Commission, delegating narrow responsibility to prevent the concentration of economic power in surface transportation.

1912   The Radio Act empowers the Secretary of Commerce to grant licenses and assign wavelengths.

1916   David Sarnoff urges the American Marconi Co. to market a "radio music box."

1918   Congress rejects Navy petition for permanent control over radio.

1919   General Electric takes over the assets of the American Marconi Co. and founds the Radio Corporation of America.

1920   The Transportation Act is the first of a series of laws to stress the control of competition under a broad "public interest" mandate.

1922   AT&T introduces "toll" radio broadcasting.

1923   Court limits the authority of the Secretary of Commerce in radio regulation to setting a wavelength.

       Federal Trade Commission begins investigation of monopoly practices in the radio industry.

1926   Court rules that Secretary of Commerce cannot refuse to grant a license and cannot limit the broadcasting power of stations. Chaos on the air waves grows worse.

       General Electric, Westinghouse, and RCA form the first radio network, NBC, and agree to lease lines from AT&T.

1927   The Columbia Phonograph Broadcasting System, later known as CBS, becomes the second radio network.

       The Radio Act establishes the Federal Radio Commission to control the chaos of the air waves.

       NBC splits into two radio networks, the Red and Blue.

1928   Davis Amendment to the Radio Act requires that radio stations be allocated among the five regional zones from which Commissioners were selected proportional to population and area.

1930   U.S. antitrust suit against RCA and its patent allies is terminated with a consent decree.

1931   Eugene MacDonald, founder of Zenith, proposes a subscription radio service.

1933   Research on FM radio conducted at RCA.

1934   The Communications Act establishes the Federal Communications Commission unifying the regulation of communications systems.

1935   Edwin Armstrong demonstrates FM radio before the Institute of Radio Engineers and receives a favorable response.

David Sarnoff commits RCA to the rapid development of a commercial television system.

1936   The Davis Amendment is repealed and replaced by a general provision to make an "equitable distribution" of radio stations throughout the United States.

1938   FCC begins its inquiry into network broadcasting.

FCC reports on the advantages of FM over AM radio.

1940   The commercial authorization of FM radio begins.

1941   FCC issues its *Report on Chain Broadcasting* requiring NBC to sell one of its networks.

FCC permits limited commercial television service in the VHF spectrum area.

1943   FCC establishes the Radio Technical Planning Board, an industry panel, to advise on postwar spectrum allocations.

Supreme Court upholds the FCC's 1941 network rules.

NBC sells the Blue network. It later becomes the ABC network.

1944   K.A. Norton, former FCC engineer recommends shift of spectrum area for FM radio from the 43–50 MHz band to the 92–106 MHz band.

1945   FCC shifts FM out of original spectrum area against the recommendations of the Radio Technical Planning Board and RCA. 500,000 receivers are made obsolete.

FCC approves the CBS-proposed "Single-Market" plan for FM radio. It lowers the antenna heights and maximum power of northeast metropolitan stations.

FCC permits AM operators to duplicate programming on FM stations.

FCC rescinds 1940 order requiring two hour daily independent programming on FM.

FCC makes available 13 VHF channels for commercial television denying CBS petition for immediate development of the UHF spectrum for color television.

1946   FCC issues "Blue Book" criticizing extensive advertising and lack of local programming in radio.

1947   Zenith proposes a subscription television service through its Phonevision system.

1948   FCC orders a freeze on new television station licensing due to overcrowding in the VHF spectrum area.

1949   First inspection of a CATV system by an FCC staff engineer.

1950   Zenith conducts subscription television tests in Chicago.

1951   CBS proposes all-UHF television for Chicago, Boston, and San Francisco markets.

President Truman establishes the Office of Telecommunications Advisor to the President.

FCC shifts the primary basis of its staff organization from professional departments (legal, engineering, and accounting) to functional bureaus (broadcast, common carrier, etc.).

1952   Zenith seeks approval for commercial subscription television.

Administrative Procedure Act establishes the position of FCC Hearing Examiner to act independently in a quasi-judicial capacity.

FCC ends television freeze with the allocation of VHF and UHF television stations to communities and reserves channels for educational use.

1953   FCC expresses concern over possible electrical interference of CATV with broadcast television.

FCC expresses concern about the impact of subscription television on the established television system.

RCA color television system accepted over that of CBS.

1954   FCC permits TV satellite-station broadcasting.

FCC increases to seven the maximum number of stations that one owner can hold provided that two are UHF stations.

1955   FCC seeks comments on the merits of subscription television.

FCC permits FM "functional" music programming through Subsidiary Communications Authorizations.

DuMont television network ceases operations.

1956   UHF station owners petition FCC to prohibit satellite-station broadcasts.

Department of Defense rejects FCC requests for more VHF space.

House Judiciary Committee proposes all-channel television legislation.

1957   FCC sets testing guidelines for subscription television.

FCC reports on the need to shift all television broadcasting to the UHF spectrum.

1958   FCC delays subscription television tests at the request of the Congress.

1959   FCC severely restricts tests of subscription television systems.

FCC declines to assume jurisdiction over CATV systems.

1960   Department of Defense again rejects FCC request for more VHF spectrum space.

FCC continues policy of reducing VHF station mileage separations in order to allow for more VHF stations.

1962   All-Channel Receiver Act requires new receivers to have full VHF and UHF capacity.

Subscription television test begins in Hartford, Connecticut.

FCC imposes restrictions on microwave systems transmitting signals to a cable system.

President Kennedy establishes the Office of Telecommunications Management within the Office of Emergency Preparedness.

1964   FCC begins to limit duplication of AM station programming on FM stations.

1965   FCC extends its jurisdiction over all microwave-fed cable systems by establishing carriage and nonduplication provisions.

1966   FCC asserts jurisdiction over all cable systems and prevents importation of distant signals into the top 100 markets without a hearing before the Commission.

1967   FCC Committee on Subscription Television supports a restricted pay system.

1968   Supreme Court affirms FCC jurisdiction over CATV and rules that such systems are not required to make copyright payments for programming.

FCC issues interim CATV rules freezing distant signal importation into top-100 markets. Accompanying report outlines vast potential for future cable systems.

FCC issues rules for subscription television setting programming restrictions and a minimum number of free broadcast hours.

1969   Appeals court affirms FCC right to rule on STV.

FCC issues further restrictions on STV sports programming.

1970   Supreme Court affirms FCC right to regulate STV programming.

President Nixon creates the Office of Telecommunications Policy.

1971   FCC issues letter of intent to rule on CATV.

1972   FCC issues Report and Order on cable television, restricting its expansion into major markets.

1974   Supreme Court rules that cable systems importing distant signals are not required to make copyright payments.

1975   FCC applies slightly more liberal subscription programming rules to pay-cable television.

1977   President Carter abolishes the Office of Telecommunications Policy, merges its functions with the Commerce Department's Office of Telecommunications and creates a new telecommunications policy-making agency in the Commerce Department, the National Telecommunications and Information Administration.

1978   House Communications Subcommittee proposes rewrite of Communications Act.

References

Agee, W.K. Cross-channel ownership of communications media. *Journalism Quarterly*, December, 1949.

Allison, G.T. *Essence of Decision: Explaining the Cuban Missile Crisis*. Boston: Little, Brown, 1971.

Archer, G. L. History of Radio: *to 1926*. New York: American Historical Society, 1938.

Archer, G. L. *Big Business and Radio*. New York: American Historical Society, 1939.

Armstrong, E.H. A method of reducing disturbances in radio signaling by a system of frequency modulation. *Proceedings of the Institute of Radio Engineers*, 1936, *24*, 689–740.

Arrow, K.J. *The Limits of Organization*. New York: Norton, 1974.

Attorney General's Committee on Administrative Procedure. *Final report*. Washington, D.C.: Government Printing Office, 1941.

Bacon, K.H., & Karr, A. The regulators: Federal commissions are masters of delay on cases before them. *Wall Street Journal*, October 9, 1974, pp. 1, 20, 21.

Baer, W.S. *Interactive television: Prospects for two-way services on cable* (R-888-MF). Santa Monica, Cal.: Rand, November 1971.

Baer, W.S. *Cable Television: Handbook for Decision-Making (R-1133-NSF)*. Santa Monica, Cal.: Rand, February 1973.

Bagdikian, B. H. *The Information Machines: Their Impact on Men and the Media*. New York: Harper & Row, 1971.

Banning, W.P. *Commercial Broadcasting Pioneer: The WEAF Experiment, 1922–26*. Cambridge, Mass.: Harvard Univ. Press, 1946.

Barnet, R.J., & Muller, R.E. *Global Reach: The Power of the Multinational Corporations*. New York: Simon & Schuster, 1974.

Barnouw, E. *A Tower in Babel: A History of Broadcasting in the United States to 1933*. New York: Oxford Univ. Press, 1966.

Barnouw, E. *The Golden Web: A History of Broadcasting in the United States, Vol. II—1933–1953*. New York: Oxford Univ. Press, 1968.

Barnouw, E. *The Image Empire: A History of Broadcasting in the United States, Vol. III—From 1953*. New York: Oxford Univ. Press, 1970.

Berner, R.O. *Constraints on the Regulatory Process: A Case Study of the Regulation of Cable Television*. Unpublished honors thesis, Harvard College, 1974.

Bernstein, M.S. The independent agency—A new scapegoat. *Yale Law Journal*, June, 1956, *65*, 1068, 1070–76.

Bernstein, M.S. *Regulating Business by Independent Commission*. Princeton, N.J.: Princeton Univ. Press, 1955.

Bliven, B. How radio is making our world. *Century, 108,* June 1924, 154.

Booz, Allen & Hamilton, Inc. *Organization and Management of the FCC.* Chicago: Booz, Allen, & Hamilton, 1962.

Borchardt, K. *Structure and Performance of the U.S. Communications Industry.* Boston: Harvard Univ. Press, 1970.

Bowers, R.T. *Television and the Public.* New York: Holt, 1973.

Branscomb, A. The TelePrompTer Syndrome. Mimeo, 1974.

Briggs, A. *The Birth of Broadcasting: The History of Broadcasting in the United Kingdom,* Vol. 1. London: Oxford Univ. Press, 1961.

Brinton, A. W. *The Regulation of Broadcasting by the FCC: A Case Study in Regulation by Independent Commission.* Unpublished doctoral dissertation, Harvard Univ., 1962.

Broadcasting Publications, Inc. *Broadcasting Yearbooks: 1939–1977.* Washington, D.C.

Brown, L. *Television: The Business Behind the Box.* New York: Harcourt, Brace, & Jovanovich, 1971.

Brown, N.K. The subscription television controversy: A continuing symptom of Federal Communications Commission ills. *Federal Communications Bar Journal, 3,* 259–282.

Business Week, March 27, 1971. The TV networks shrug off new competition. Pp. 90–96.

Canon, B.C. Voting behavior on the FCC. *Midwest Journal of Political Science,* 1969, *13,* 593–594.

Capron, W.M. (Ed.). *Technological Changes in Regulated Industries.* Washington, D.C.: Brookings Institution, 1971.

Cary, W. *Politics and the Regulatory Agencies.* New York: McGraw-Hill, 1967.

Chandler, A.D., Jr. *Strategy and Structure: Chapters in the History of the American Industrial Enterprise.* Cambridge, Mass.: MIT Press, 1962.

Chase, F., Jr. *Sound and Fury.* New York: Harper, 1942.

Chazen, L., & Ross, L. Federal regulation of cable television: The visible hand. *Harvard Law Review,* 1970, *83,* 1828 ff.

Cheek, L. III, An analysis of proposals to deregulate commercial radio broadcasting. *Federal Communications Bar Journal,* 1972, *25,* 1–52.

Cherington, P.W., Hirsch, L.V., & Brandwein, R. (Eds.). *Television Station Ownership.* New York: Hastings House, 1971.

Coase, R. The Federal Communications Commission. *Journal of Law and Economics,* October 1959, *2,* 1–40.

Coase, R. The economics of broadcasting and public policy. In P.W. MacAvoy (Ed.), *The Crisis of the Regulatory Commissions.* New York: Norton, 1970. pp. 95–96.

Coase, R., & Barrett, W. *Educational TV: Who Should Pay?* Washington, D.C.: American Enterprise Institute for Public Policy Research, 1968.

Comaner, W.S., & Mitchell, B.M. The costs of planning: The FCC and cable television. *Journal of Law and Economics,* April 1952, *15,* No. 1, 177–206.

Committee for Economic Development. *Broadcasting and Cable Television: Policies for Diversity and Change.* New York: C.E.D., 1975.

Cotter, C. *Government and Private Enterprise.* New York: Holt, Rinehart and Winston, 1960.

Cox, K.A. Does the FCC really do anything? *Journal of Broadcasting,* Spring, 1967, *11,* No. 2, 97–113.

Cox, K.A. What it's like inside the FCC. *Telephony,* September 5, 1970.

Cushman, R. *Independent Regulatory Commissions.* New York: Oxford Univ. Press, 1941.

Cyert, R.M., & March, J.G. *A Behavioral Theory of the Firm.* Englewood Cliffs, N.J.: Prentice-Hall, 1963.

Davis, H.P. The early history of broadcasting in the United States. In *The Radio Industry.* Chicago: Shaw, 1928.

Davis, L.E., & North, D.C. *Institutional Change and American Economic Growth*. Cambridge, England: Cambridge Univ. Press, 1971.

Davis, S. *The Law of Radio Communication*. New York: McGraw-Hill, 1927.

de Forest, L. *Father of Radio*. Chicago: Wilcox & Follett, 1950.

Doerfer, J. S. Community antenna television systems. *Federal Communications Bar Journal*, 1955, *14*, 4–14.

Downs, A. *Inside Bureaucracy*. Boston: Little, Brown, 1967.

Eckert, R.D. Spectrum allocation and regulatory incentives. *Proceedings of the Office of Telecommunications Policy Conference on Communications Policy Research*. Washington, D.C.: Office of Telecommunications Policy, 1972.

Edelman, M. *The Licensing of Radio Services in the United States, 1927 to 1947: A Study in Administrative Formulation of Policy*. Urbana, Ill.: Univ. of Illinois Press, 1950.

Electronics Industry Association. The Future of Broadband Communications: The IED/EIA Response to Federal Communications Docket No. 18397, Part V. October 29, 1969.

Emery, F.E., & Trist, E.L. The causal texture of organizational environments. *Human Relations*, 1965, *18*, 21–32.

Emery, W.B. *Broadcasting and Government: Responsibilities and Regulation*. Michigan State Univ. Press, 1971.

Fainsod, M., Gordon, L., & Palamountain, J.C. *Government and the American economy*, 3rd ed. New York: Norton, 1959.

Feldman, N.E. *The Potential Role of Cable Television in the Wideband Distribution System*. Santa Monica, Cal.: Rand, 1970.

Fortune, October 1939. Revolution in radio. pp. 86–87.

Friendly, F.W. *Due to Circumstances Beyond Our Control*. New York: Vintage, 1967.

Friendly, H.J. *The Federal Administrative Agencies*. Cambridge, Mass.: Harvard Univ. Press, 1962.

Frost, S.E., Jr. *Education's Own Stations: The History of Broadcast Licenses Issued to Educational Institutions*. Chicago: Univ. of Chicago Press, 1937.

Galbraith, J.K. *The Great Crash*. New York: Houghton Mifflin, 1955.

Geller, H. A modest proposal to reform the Federal Communications Commission. *Georgetown Law Journal*, 1975, *63*, 705.

Giraud, D., Garrison, G., & Willis, E.E. *Television and Radio*, 4th ed. New York: Appleton-Century-Crofts, 1971.

Goldhamer, H. *The Social Effects of Communication Technology* (R-486-RSF). Santa Monica, Cal.: Rand, May 1970.

Gulick, L. Notes on the theory of organization. In L. Gulick & L. Urwick (Eds.), *The Elements of Administration*. New York: Harper, 1945.

Haas, J.E., & Drabek, T.E. *Complex Organizations: A Sociological Perspective*. New York: MacMillan, 1973.

Head, S.W. *Broadcasting in America*, 2nd ed. Boston: Houghton Mifflin, 1972.

Herbers, J. Nixon's imprint deep at regulatory agencies. *The New York Times*, May 6, 1973.

Herring, E.P. Politics and radio regulation. *Harvard Business Review*, 1935, *13*, No. 2, 167–178.

Herring, E.P. *Federal commissioners: A study of their careers and qualifications*. Cambridge, Mass.: Harvard Univ. Press, 1936a.

Herring, E.P. *Public administration and the public interest*. New York: McGraw-Hill, 1936.

Holt, D. The origin of "public interest" in Broadcasting. *Educational Broadcasting Review*, 1967, *1*, No. 1, 15–19.

Jackson, J.H., Should radio be used for advertising? *Radio Broadcast*, 1922, *2*, 72.

Jaffe, L. The effective limits of the administrative process: A reevaluation. *Harvard Law Review*, 1954, *67*, 1105, 1109.

Jaffe, L. WHDH: The FCC and broadcasting license renewals. *Harvard Law Review*, 1969, *82*, 1693, 1700.

Johnson, L.L. *Cable Television and the Question of Protecting Local Broadcasting* (R-595-MF). Santa Monica, Cal.: Rand, October 1970.

Johnson, N. *How to Talk Back to Your Television Set.* New York: Bantam, 1970.

Johnson, N. A new fidelity to the regulatory ideal. *Georgetown Law Journal,* 1971, *59,* 883–884.

Johnson, N. The why of public broadcasting. *Educational Broadcasting Review,* 1967, *1,* No. 2, 5–10.

Jome, H.L. *Economics of the Radio Industry.* Chicago: Shaw, 1925.

Kahn, A.E. *The Economics of Regulation: Principles and Institutions, Vol. 2: Institutional Issues.* New York: Wiley, 1971.

Kahn, F.J. Economic injury and the public interest. *Federal Communications Bar Journal,* 1969, *23,* No. 3, Pt. I, 182–201.

Kahn, F.J. (Ed.). *Documents of American Broadcasting.* New York: Appleton-Century-Crofts, 1973.

Kahn, F.J. The quasi-utility basis for broadcast regulation. *Journal of Broadcasting,* 1974, *18,* No. 3, 259–276.

Katz, D., & Kahn, R.L. *The Social Psychology of Organizations.* New York: Wiley, 1965.

Keehn, D. A Short Review of the Development of Cable Television to 1973. Public Affairs Paper No. 2. Seattle: Univ. of Washington, 1973.

Kittross, J.M. Television Frequency Allocation Policy in the United States. Unpublished doctoral dissertation. Ann Arbor, Michigan: University Microfilms, 1960.

Krasnow, E.G., & Longley, L.D. *The Politics of Broadcast Regulation.* New York: St. Martin's, 1973.

Krasnow, E.G., & Shooshan, III, H.M. Congressional oversight: The ninety-second congress and the Federal Communications Commission. *Harvard Journal on Legislation,* 1973, *10,* No. 2, 297–329.

Krislov, S., & Musolf, L.D. (Eds.) *The Politics of Regulation.* Boston: Houghton Mifflin, 1964.

Kuhn, T.S. *The Structure of Scientific Revolutions,* 2nd ed. Chicago, Ill.: Univ. of Chicago Press, 1970.

Landis, J.M. *Report on Regulatory Agencies to the President-Elect.* Washington, D.C.: December, 1960.

Le Duc, D.R. The FCC v. CATV et al.: A theory of regulatory reflex action. *Federal Communications Bar Journal,* 1969, *23,* No. 2, 93–109.

Le Duc, D.R. *Cable Television and the FCC: A Crisis in Media Control.* Philadelphia, Pa.: Temple Univ. Press, 1973.

Lees, F.A., & Yang, C.Y. The redistribution effects of television advertising. *The Economic Journal,* June 1966, *76,* 302, 499–507.

Lessing, L. The television freeze. *Fortune,* November 1949, *40,* 123–127, 157–168.

Lessing, L. Cinderella in the sky. *Fortune,* October 1967, 131–133, 196–208.

Lessing, L. *Man of High Fidelity: Edwin Howard Armstrong.* New York: Bantam, 1969.

Levin, H.J. *Broadcast Regulation and Joint Ownership of Media.* New York: NYU Press, 1960.

Levin, H.J. Competition, diversity, and the television group ownership rule. *Columbia Law Review,* May 1970, *70,* 791–835.

Levin, H.J. *The Invisible Resource: Use and Regulation of the Radio Spectrum.* Baltimore, Md.: Johns Hopkins, 1971.

Lewis, A. To regulate the regulators. In S. Krislov & L.D. Musolf (Eds.), *The Politics of Regulation.* Boston, Mass.: Houghton Mifflin, 1964.

Lichty, L. Members of the Federal Radio Commission and the FCC: 1927–61. *Journal of Broadcasting,* Winter 1961–1962, *6,* 23–34.

Lichty, L. The impact of FRC and FCC commissioners' backgrounds on the regulation of broadcasting. *Journal of Broadcasting,* Spring 1962, *6,* 97–109.

Lindblom, C.E. The science of muddling through. *Public Administration Review,* 1959, *19,* No. 2, 79–88.

Loevinger, L. Regulation and competition as alternatives. *Antitrust Bulletin,* 1966, *11*, 101–115.

Longley, L.D. The FM shift in 1945, *Journal of Broadcasting,* Fall 1968, *12,* 353–365.

MacAvoy, P.W. (Ed.). *The Crisis of the Regulatory Commissions.* New York: Norton, 1970.

MacGregor, J. Pay-TV may hold key to cable-TV's future in vast urban market. *Wall Street Journal,* May 17, 1973, pp. 1, 27.

MacLaurin, W.R. *Invention and Innovation in the Radio Industry.* New York: MacMillan, 1949.

Maddox, B. *Beyond Babel: New Directions in Communications.* New York: Simon & Schuster, 1972.

Martin, J. *Future Developments in Telecommunications.* Englewood, N.J.: Prentice-Hall, 1971.

Marx, K., & Engels, F. In R. Pascal (Ed.), *The German Ideology.* New York: International Publishers, 1947.

Mason, W.F., et al. *Urban Cable Systems.* Washington, D.C.: Mitre, 1972.

Mayer, M. *About Television.* New York: Harper & Row, 1972.

Meyer, C. The preteen market. *Television Magazine,* 1967, *24,* No. 7, 37.

Michael, J.R. (Ed.). *Working on the System.* New York: Basic Books, 1974.

Minasian, J.R. Television pricing and the theory of public goods. *Journal of Law and Economics,* October 1964, *7,* 71–80.

Minow, N. *Equal Time: The Private Broadcaster and the Public Interest.* New York: Atheneum, 1964.

Moore, Jr., B.C. The FCC: Competition and communication. In J. Green (Ed.), *The Monopoly Makers.* New York: Grossman, 1973. Pp. 35–73.

Mosco, V. *The Regulation of Broadcasting in the United States: A Comparative Analysis.* Cambridge, Mass.: Harvard University Program on Information Technologies and Public Policy, 1975.

Noll, R.G. The behavior of regulatory agencies. *Review of Social Economy,* 1971, *29,* No. 1, 15–19. (a)

Noll, R.G. (Ed.). *Reforming Regulation: Studies in the Regulation of Economic Activity.* Washington, D.C.: The Brookings Institution, 1971. (b)

Noll, R.G., Peck, M.J., & McGowan, J.J. *Economic Aspects of Television Regulation.* Washington, D.C.: The Brookings Institution, 1973.

Owen, B.M. Beebe, J.H., & Manning, W.G. *Television Economics.* Lexington, Mass.: Heath, 1974.

Owen, B.M. A view from the President's Office of Telecommunications Policy. In R.E. Park (Ed.), *The Role of Analysis in Regulatory Decisionmaking.* Lexington, Mass.: Heath, 1973.

Padden, P.R. The emerging role of citizens' groups in broadcast regulation. *Federal Communications Bar Journal,* 1972, *25,* No. 2, 82–110.

Park, R.E. *Potential Impact of Cable Growth on Television Broadcasting* (R-587-FF). Santa Monica, Cal.: Rand, October 1970.

Park, R.E. *Cable Television and UHF Broadcasting* (R-689-MF). Santa Monica, Cal.: Rand, January, 1971.

Park, R.E. *The Exclusivity Provisions of the Federal Communications Commission's Cable Television Regulations* (R-1057-FF/MF). Santa Monica, Cal.: Rand, 1972.

Park, R.E. (Ed.). *The Role of Analysis in Regulatory Decisionmaking: The Case of Cable Television.* Lexington, Mass.: Heath, 1973.

Paulu, B. *Radio and Television Broadcasting on the European Continent.* Minneapolis, Minn.: Univ. of Minnesota Press, 1967.

Pennybacker, J.H., & Braden, W.W. (Eds.). *Broadcasting and the Public Interest.* New York: Random House, 1969.

Powledge, F. *Public Television: A Question of Survival.* Washington, D.C.: Public Affairs Press, 1972.

The President's Advisory Council on Executive Organization. *A New Regulatory Framework: Report on Selected Independent Regulatory Agencies* (The Ash Report). Washington, D.C.: U.S. Government Printing Office, January 30, 1971.

The President's Committee on Administrative Management. *Report of the Committee with Studies of Administrative Management in the Federal Government*. Washington, D.C.: U.S. Government Printing Office, 1937.

President's Communication Policy Board. *Telecommunications: A Program for Progress*. Washington, D.C.: U.S. Government Printing Office, 1951.

President's Task Force on Telecommunications. *Final Report*. Washington, D.C.: U.S. Government Printing Office, 1969.

Price, M., & Wicklein, J. *Cable Television: A Guide for Citizen Action*. Philadelphia, Pa.: Pilgrim Press, 1972.

Radio Broadcast, May 1922. Radio currents: An editorial interpretation. Pp. 1–4.

Rivkin, S.R. *Cable Television: A Guide to Federal Regulation*. Santa Monica, Ca.: Rand, 1973.

Rorty, J. The impending radio war. *Harpers*, 1931, *163*, 713.

Rorty, J. *Our Master's Voice: Advertising*. New York: John Day, 1934.

Schiller, H.I. *Mass Communications and American Empire*. New York: Kelley, 1970.

Schmeckebier, L.F. *The F.R.C.: Its History, Activities and Organization*. Washington, D.C.: Brookings Institution, 1932.

Schurmann, F. *Ideology and Organization in Communist China*, 2nd ed. Berkeley, Cal.: Univ. of California Press, 1971.

Schwartz, B. *The Professor and the Commissions*. New York: Knopf, 1959.

Seiden, M.H. *An Economic Analysis of Community Antenna Television Stations and the Television Broadcasting Industry*. Report to the Federal Communications Commission, Washington, D.C., 1965.

Seiden, M.H. *Cable Television U.S.A.: An Analysis of Government Policy*. New York: Praeger, 1972.

Shurick, E.P.J. *The First Quarter-Century of American Broadcasting*. Kansas City: Midland, 1946.

Siepmann, C.A. *Radio's Second Chance*. Boston: Little, Brown, 1946.

Simon, H.A. *Administrative Behavior*. New York: MacMillan, 1957.

Simon, S.S. *Crisis in Television: A Study of the Private Judgment and the Public Interest*. New York: Living Books, 1966.

Skornia, H.J. *Television and Society: An Inquest and Agenda for Improvement*. New York: McGraw-Hill, 1965.

Sloan Commission on Cable Communications. *On the Cable: The Television of Abundance*. New York: McGraw-Hill, 1971.

Smith, A. Cash on the air. *New Society*, June 20, 1974, *128*, No. 611, 713.

Smith, R.L. *The Wired Nation: Cable TV—The Electronic Communications Highway*. New York: Harper & Row, 1972.

Special Committee on Administrative Law. Report before the 57th annual meeting of the American Bar Association. Milwaukee, Wisc., 1934.

Spievack, E.B. Presidential assault on telecommunications. *The Federal Communications Bar Journal*, 1969, *23*, No. 3, Pt. 1, 155–181.

Stavins, R.L., & Fellows of the Institute for Policy Studies. *Television Today: The End of Communication and the Death of Community*. Washington, D.C.: Institute for Policy Studies, 1969.

Steinbruner, H.D. *The Cybernetic Theory of Decision: New Dimensions of Political Analysis*. Princeton, N.J.: Princeton Univ. Press, 1974.

Sterling, C. Second Service: A history of Commerical FM Broadcasting to 1969. Unpublished doctoral dissertation. Ann Arbor, Michigan: University Microfilms, 1969.

Sterling, C. Second service: Some keys to the development of FM broadcasting. *Journal of Broadcasting*, 1971, *15*, No. 2, 181–194.

Stern, R.H., Regulatory influences upon television's development: Early years under the Federal Radio Commission. *American Journal of Economics and Sociology*, 1963, *22*, 347–362.(a)

Stern, R.H., Television in the thirties. *American Journal of Economics and Sociology,* 1964, *23,* 285–301.(b)

Taylor, T.F. (Ed.). *Radio as a Cultural Agency.* Washington, D.C.: National Committee on Education by Radio, 1934.

Television Digest, July 26, 1965. CATV: The communications revolution.

Television Factbook, 1969–1977, Nos. 39–46. Washington, D.C.: Television Digest, Inc.

Udy, S. *Work in Traditional and Modern Society.* Englewood Cliffs, N.J.: Prentice Hall, 1970.

U.S. Commission on Organization of the Executive Branch of the Government, Committee on Independent Regulatory Commissions. *Task Force Report for the Hoover Commission: Staff Report on the FCC.* Washington, D.C.: U.S. Government Printing Office, 1948.

U.S. Commission of Organization of the Executive Branch of the Government, Committee on Independent Regulatory Commissions. *A Report with Recommendations* (The first Hoover Commission report). Washington, D.C.: U.S. Government Printing Office, 1949.

U.S. Commission on Organization of the Executive Branch of the Government. *Legal Services and Procedure.* Washington, D.C.: U.S. Government Printing Office, 1955.

U.S. Congress, House. *H.R. 8014: A Bill to Amend the Federal Communications Commission and Revise Its Procedures so as to Permit the Commission to More Effectively Perform Its Duties.* 94th Cong., 1st Sess., June 18, 1975.

U.S. Congress, House, Committee on Interstate and Foreign Commerce. *Hearings on H.J.R. 78.* 80th Cong., 2d Sess. 1948.

U.S. Congress, House, Committee on Interstate and Foreign Commerce. *Administrative Process and Ethical Questions.* 85th Cong., 2d Sess. 1958. (a)

U.S. Congress, House, Committee on Interstate and Foreign Commerce. *Hearings on Subscription Television.* 85th Cong., 2d Sess. 1958. (b)

U.S. Congress, House, Committee on Interstate and Foreign Commerce. *Network Broadcasting.* 85th Cong., 2d Sess. 1958. (c)

U.S. Congress, House, Committee on Interstate and Foreign Commerce. *Regulation of Broadcasting: Half a Century of Government Regulation of Broadcasting and the Need for Further Legislative Action—A Study for the Committee.* 85th Cong., 2d Sess., 1958. (d)

U.S. Congress, House, Committee on Interstate and Foreign Commerce. *All-Channel Television Receivers and Deintermixture.* 87th Cong., 2d Sess. 1962.

U.S. Congress, House, Committee on Interstate and Foreign Commerce. *Regulation of Community Antenna Television: Hearings on H.R. 7715.* 89th Cong., 1st Sess., 1965.

U.S. Congress, House, Committee on Interstate and Foreign Commerce. *Subscription Television: Hearings . . . on H.R. 12435—A Bill to Amend the Communications Acts of 1934 so as to Prohibit the Granting of Authority to Broadcast Pay Television Programs.* 90th Cong., 1st Sess. 1967.

U.S. Congress, House, Committee on Interstate and Foreign Commerce. *Hearings on H.R. 420 (and Related Bills): To Amend the Communications Act of 1934 so as to Prohibit the Granting of Authority to Broadcast Pay TV Programs.* 91st Cong., 1st Sess. 1969.

U.S. Congress, House, Subcommittee on Legislative Oversight of the Committee on Interstate and Foreign Commerce. *Staff Report on the Independent Regulatory Commissions.* 86th Cong., 1st Sess. 1960.

U.S. Congress, House, Committee on the Judiciary. *Report of the Antitrust Subcommittee Pursuant to House Resolution 607 on the Television Broadcasting Industry.* 85th Cong., 1st. Sess. 1957.

U.S. Congress, House, Committee on Merchant Marine and Fisheries. *Government Control of Radio Communications.* 65th Cong., 3d Sess. 1918.

U.S. Congress, House, Committee on Merchant Marine and Fisheries. *Jurisdiction of the Radio Commission.* 70th Cong., 1st Sess. 1928.

U.S. Congress, Senate, Committee on Interstate and Foreign Commerce. *Radio Control.* 69th Cong., 1st Sess. 1926.

U.S. Congress, Senate, Committee on Interstate and Foreign Commerce. *Hearings . . . on the Confirmation of the Federal Radio Commissioners.* 70th Cong., 1st Sess. 1928.

U.S. Congress, Senate, Committee on Interstate and Foreign Commerce. *Hearings on S. 6.* 71st Cong., 1929–30.

U.S. Congress, Senate, Committee on Interstate and Foreign Commerce. *Development of Television.* 76th Cong., 3d. Sess. 1940.

U.S. Congress, Senate, Committee on Interstate and Foreign Commerce. *Hearings on the Nominations of Wayne Coy and George E. Sterling to the FCC.* 80th Cong., 2d. Sess. 1948. (a)

U.S. Congress, Senate, Committee on Interstate and Foreign Commerce. *Hearings on the Progress of FM Radio.* 80th Cong., 2d Sess. 1948. (b)

U.S. Congress, Senate Committee on Interstate and Foreign Commerce. *Hearings on S. 3095* (The Potter Hearings). 83rd Cong., 2d Sess. 1954.

U.S. Congress, Senate Committee on Interstate and Foreign Commerce. *Investigation of Television Networks and the UHF–VHF Problem: Report of Minority Counsel.* 84th Cong., 1st Sess. 1955. (a)

U.S. Congress, Senate, Committee on Interstate and Foreign Commerce. *Television Network Regulation and the UHF Problem: Memorandum by Harry M. Plotkin.* 84th Cong., 1st Sess. 1955. (b)

U.S. Congress, Senate, Committee on Interstate and Foreign Commerce. *Hearings on S.R. 13 and 163.* (The Television Inquiry). 84th Cong., 2d. Sess. 1956. (a)

U.S. Congress, Senate, Committee on Interstate and Foreign Commerce. *The Network Monopoly: Report Prepared by Senator John W. Bricker.* 84th Cong., 2d Sess. 1956. (b)

U.S. Congress, Senate, Committee on Interstate and Foreign Commerce. *Allocation of TV Channels: Report of the Ad Hoc Advisory Committee on Allocations.* 85th Cong., 2d Sess. 1958. (a)

U.S. Congress, Senate, Committee on Interstate and Foreign Commerce. *Report on Allocations* (The Bowles Report). 85th Cong., 2d Sess. 1958. (b)

U.S. Congress, Senate, Committee on Interstate and Foreign Commerce. *Review of Allocation Problems of TV Services to Small Communities.* 85th Cong., 2d Sess. 1958. (c)

U.S. Congress, Senate, Committee on Interstate and Foreign Commerce. *Licensing of Community Antenna Television Systems.* 86th Cong., 1st Sess. 1959. (a)

U.S. Congress, Senate, Committee on Interstate and Foreign Commerce. *UHF Booster and Community Antenna Legislation.* 86th Cong., 1st Sess. 1959. (b)

U.S. Congress, Senate. *Report of the Special Committee to Study Problems of American Small Business.* 79th Cong., 2d Sess. 1944.

U.S. Federal Radio Commission. *Annual Reports of the Federal Radio Commission: 1927–1933.* Washington, D.C.: U.S. Government Printing Office.

U.S. Federal Communications Commission. *Annual Reports of the Federal Communications Commission: 1934–1974.* Washington, D.C.: U.S. Government Printing Office.

U.S. Federal Communications Commission. *Report on Frequency Modulation.* Docket 5805, May 20, 1940.

U.S. Federal Communications Commission. *Report on Chain Broadcasting.* (1941).

U.S. Federal Communications Commission. *Statement on FM Broadcast Service.* Docket 6651, January 15, 1945. (a)

U.S. Federal Communications Commission. *Final Report on Allocations from 25,000 Kc to 30,000,000 Kc.* Docket 6651, May 25, 1945. (b)

U.S. Federal Communications Commission. *Report on Allocations from 44 to 108 Megacycles.* Docket 6651, June 27, 1945. (c)

U.S. Federal Communications Commission. *Statement of FM Broadcast Service.* Docket 6651, January 15, 1945. (a)

U.S. Federal Communications Commission. *Public Service Responsibility of Broadcast Licensees.* 1946.

U.S. Federal Communications Commission. *Sixth Report on Television Allocations*. In Pike and Fisher, *Radio Regulation, 91*, May 12, 1952, at 614.

U.S. Federal Communications Commission. *Notice of Proposed Rulemaking (on Subscription Television)*. Docket 11279, 1955.

U.S. Federal Communications Commission. *In the Matter of Amendment of Part 15 of the Commission's rules Governing Restricted Radiation Devices*. In Pike and Fisher *Radio Regulation, 13*, 1956, at 1546.

U.S. Federal Communications Commission. *First report on subscription television*. In Pike and Fisher *Radio Regulation, 16*, 1957, at 1509. (a)

U.S. Federal Communications Commission. *Subscription Television Service: Notice of Further Proceedings, 22, Federal Register*, 1957, at 3759. (b)

U.S. Federal Communications Commission. *CATV and Repeater Services*. 26 FCC, 403, 1959. (a)

U.S. Federal Communications Commission. *In the Matter of Inquiring into the Impact of Community Antenna . . . on the Orderly Development of Television Broadcasting*. In Pike and Fisher *Radio Regulation, 18*, 1959, at 1573. (b)

U.S. Federal Communications Commission. *Report and Statement of Policy re Commission en banc Programming Inquiry. 25, Federal Register* August 1960, at 7298.

U.S. Federal Communications Commission. *Carter Mountain Transmission Corp*. 32 FCC, 459, 1962.

U.S. Federal Communications Commission. *First Report and Order (on Cable Television)*. 38 FCC, 683, 1965. (a)

U.S. Federal Communications Commission. *Policy Statement on Comparative Broadcast Hearings*. In Pike and Fisher *Radio Regulation, 5*, 1965 at 1901. (b).

U.S. Federal Communications Commission. *The Second Report and Order*. 2 FCC, 2d, 725, 1966.

U.S. Federal Communications Commission. *Suburban Cable Television*. 9 FCC, 2d, 1015, 1967.

U.S. Federal Communications Commission. *Fourth Report and Order (on Subscription Television)*. 15 FCC, 2d, 466, 1968. (a)

U.S. Federal Communications Commission. *Notice of Inquiry and Notice of Proposed Rulemaking*. Docket 18397, 15 FCC, 2d, 417, 1968. (b)

U.S. Federal Communications Commission. *Report of the Land Mobile Frequency Relief Committee*. 1968. (c)

U.S. Federal Communications Commission. *The Economics of the TV-CATV Interface*. Washington, D.C.: Research Branch, Broadcast Bureau, 1970. (a).

U.S. Federal Communications Commission. *Third Report and Order*. In Pike and Fisher *Radio Regulation, 24*, 2d, June 1970, at 1501. (b).

U.S. Federal Communications Commission. *Cable Television Report and Order*. 36 FCC 2d, 143, 1972. (a).

U.S. Federal Communications Commission. *Notice of Proposed Rulemaking and Memorandum, Opinion, and Order*. Dockets 19554, 18397, 18893, 1972. (b).

U.S. Federal Communications Commission. *Opinion of Commissioner Nicholas Johnson Concurring in Part and Dissenting in Part*. In re: Docket Numbers 18397, 18397-A, 18373, 18415, 18892, and 18894, 1972. (c)

U.S. Federal Communications Commission. *First Report and Order (on Pay-Cable)*. 52 FCC, 2d, 369, 1975.

U.S. Federal Trade Commission. *Report of the Federal Trade Commission on the Radio Industry*. Washington, D.C.: Government Printing Office, 1924.

U.S. Office of Telecommunications Management. *The Radio Frequency Spectrum: United States Use and Management*. Washington, D.C.: U.S. Government Printing Office, 1969.

U.S. Office of Telecommunications Policy. *The Radio Frequency Spectrum: United States Use and Management*. Washington, D.C.: U.S. Government Printing Office, January, 1973.

Warner, H.P. *Radio and Television Law.* New York: Bender, 1948.

Webbink, D.W. The impact of UHF promotion: The all-channel receiver law. *Law and Contemporary Social Problems,* Summer 1969, *34.*

Webbink, D.W. The budget priorities of the Federal Communications Commission: A note. *Federal Communications Bar Journal,* 1972, *25,* 53–65.

Wilson, J.Q. The dead hand of regulation. *The Public Interest,* Fall, 1971, *25,* 39–58.

Woodward, J. *Industrial Organization.* London: Oxford Univ. Press, 1965.

Young, J.C. How will you have your advertising? *Radio Broadcast,* December, 1924, *6.*

Zwerman, W.L. *New Perspectives on Organization Theory.* Westport, Conn.: Greenwood, 1970.

Author Index

Subject Index